D1236575

THE
AMERICAN
NANNY

ISBN 0-9615754-7-6
Library of Congress Number 85-51992
First Printing, November, 1985

Published by
TAN Press
P.O. Box 3721
Georgetown Station
Washington, D.C. 20007

For my family—
David, Diana, Russell, Rick, and Bernie

Acknowledgements

I would like to express my sincere appreciation to the following people: Bernard Landry, for his loving support and encouragement; Courtney Hagner for her advice, understanding, and professional support; Ruth Zaslow and Cathy Bowes, for teaching me how to write; Renee Simms, Al Sacharov, and Dan Poynter, who helped me to understand publishing; and to the contributing authors Deborah Davis, Judith Bunge, and Miriam Freilicher.

CONTENTS

CHAPTER 1

THE AMERICAN NANNY MARKET

Until just a few years ago, the word "nanny" brought images of the magical Mary Poppins flying in on her umbrella. For many families today, the nanny is no longer a fantasy character, but a vital part of their childrearing plan. If fictional characters are to set the stage, however, I would instead choose Julie Andrews as she appeared in *The Sound of Music*. Like Mary Poppins, Julie gave an entertaining song and dance, but she also dealt with nightmares, growing pains, and a whistle-blowing father. She helped the children feel good about themselves and played a loving but firm role in their lives.

Other television shows like "Family Affair" with Mr. French, "Andy Griffith" with Aunt Bea, and more recently "Charles In Charge" featuring a living-in college student[1], all portray very different, but viable options for in-home childcare. How many mothers have watched these shows and said "I wish I had a Mr. French myself"?

What parents are really saying is that today we want our childcare to be the closest thing to the *real* thing. We want surrogate parents, both mothers and fathers, to take our place in the home for the eight to twelve hours per day

[1]. While not common, some men do become nannies. I use the female pronoun when refering to nannies as it is largely women who enter the profession.

that we are away. We want someone to love our children as we do, and to build a sound and loving relationship with them.

We are seeking those who, like ourselves, are educated, creative, and responsible; those who come from a similar cultural background; those who can provide a type of "extended family" relationship, while still maintaining their professionalism.

This book is meant to guide both families and care providers through the in-home childcare search and relationship. While many of these guidelines pertain to both the trained and untrained childcare provider, I restrict my use of the term "nanny" to those providing professional care (as I have defined it on page 3). The guidelines I present are not hard and fast rules. They are simply ideas that have worked for me as a nanny, a nanny recruiter, and a family placement counselor.

Who Is Hiring The American Nanny?

The American nanny is a new phenonena riding the wave of professional women entering the workforce. We have many other childcare options, including day care centers, day care mothers, and babysitters. The vast number of children requiring quality care however, makes that care difficult, if not impossible to find. In light of this, many families are finding the professional nanny a promising option.

Today, it is the dual-career family which constitutes the majority of those seeking the American nanny. While many of these families must carefully budget to afford the nanny, the quality care she provides is considered worth the cost. Of course, multi-millionare families with three homes and a private jet hire nannies too. However, working for these families is not always the Harlequin romance novel one might think it would be. As Deborah Davis of the National Nanny Newsletter writes:

"Work as a nanny, whether in a castle or in a cottage, is still hard work. A professional nanny is on duty most of the time taking care of children whether they are in the Bahamas or in Burbank, and caring for children properly is physically, emotionally, and mentally taxing."[2]

Defining Professional Childcare

The term "nanny" is used loosely in the U.S., at least in comparison to its traditional use in Europe, where the true professional nanny has been trained in accord with much more rigorous standards. In fact, in Europe "nanny" was the name a child called his Nursery Nurse (her true title). In the United States, where the trained Nursery Nurse is scarce, our many different versions of this in-home childcare person are all beginning to fall under the title of "nanny". Childcare providers with neither education nor training are calling themselves nannies, while those trained or educated are often referred to as "professional nannies".

While there are no official definitions, we at Nanny Placement Services, Inc. have defined professional childcare as: "the active involvement in the physical, intellectual, emotional, and social growth and well-being of the child." The professional will have both the desire and ability to perform this role in a child's life, no matter where she has attained the education and skills to perform this role.

Standards in the U.S. are currently being set so that education and training become a prerequisite to the status of professional, as in any other occupation. Many educators of nannies feel that looking at England's current Nursery Nurse Examination Board (N.N.E.B.) regulations can help to define what qualifications and training a nanny

[2]. National Nanny Newsletter, Volume 1, Number Four, July 1985.

needs in order to be considered a professional. However, it is obvious that we will need to adjust the cultural elements of any training to those of the American family and lifestyle.

The NNEB graduate must pass an examination by showing a thorough knowledge of the following subjects:[3]

★ **Growth and Development,** including stages of development and observations.

★ **Physical Development and Keeping Children Healthy,** including promotion and maintenance of health, surveillance programs, safety in the environment, clothing and footwear, baby equipment, nutrition, childhood illnesses and ailments, first aid, care of the sick child, and development deviations.

★ **Cognitive Development and Learning Through Play,** including stimulation, sensory development, development of skills, speech and language development, activities, and organization and provision of materials and equipment.

★ **Emotional Development,** including stimulation, bonding, parent/child relationships, family relations, emotional expression, self awareness, loss and grief, and "other deprivations."

★ **Social Relationships,** including role and role conflict, the family as a social institution, the family in the community, differing cultural and sub-cultural patterns of family functioning, and deviations in family functioning.

★ **Rights and Responsibilities of Children and the Family,** including the rights and responsibilities of individuals in society, legislative and administrative framework, statutory and voluntary services to families with young children, and social deviance.

---

[3]. National Nursury Examination Board, Regulations Guide on the content of courses leading to the award of the NNEB Certificate.

4

★ **The Nursery Nurse in Employment,** including the meaning of professionalism, relationships between occupational groups, working with managers, relationships between employer and employees, the role of the nursery nurse in the public sector and the role of the nursery nurse in the private sector.

★ *In addition,* these specific areas of knowledge must be complimented by other broader studies, including such subjects as communications and other creative arts, man and his environment, living in society and hands-on, practical experience with children.

At this point, no one can predict whether the two year community college program or the private eight- to twelve-week intensive, practical training course will set the professional standards for the U.S. It is obvious however that those with a well-rounded education and in-home childcare training are more desirable that those without, assuming that their training has not made them inflexible to the everyday work required in the American family's home.

The Pro's and Con's of In-Home Childcare

While many families feel that in-home childcare is the best available arrangement, there are positive and negative aspects to both the work and personal relationships. Families considering the in-home childcare relationship for the first time should consider their specific needs and abilities in relation to the following pro's and con's.

THE PRO'S
Flexibility—Many families need the flexibility of the in-home childcare provider. Unlike day care centers or mothers, the private home does not "close" at 6 pm. The

in-home relationship can give parents peace of mind when the unexpected arises.

Stability—One of the greatest advantages of in-home childcare is the stability factor. While turnover is high in *any* kind of child care, public or private, the home environment gives the child stability. Because he naps in his own bed, plays with his own toys, and continues his regular diet, a child will often feel less disrupted when the nanny fills in for his parents than he would if he were dropped off at a school for 12 hours each day.

Time Saving—Providing the nanny is always prompt, it is much easier for children to stay at home than to commute with parents to another home or day care center. Parents can spend more time getting themselves ready for their day while the nanny readies the children.

Quality Control—In your home, you set the standards. Discipline, nutrition, and educational activities are all under the individual family's control. While monitoring takes active involvement, children benefit from the consistency between parent and nanny.

Personal Attention—While day care mothers and day care centers must keep under certain teacher-student ratios, these ratios can be as high as eight or even ten children per staff member. At home, the nanny can provide much more individualized and quality care.

Infant Care—It is almost impossible to find quality infant care based outside of the home. Most day care centers do not accept infants, and those that do often have poor teacher-infant ratios. Day care mothers, often caring for several children, usually cannot spend an adequate amount of time with an infant. Even if there are other siblings in the home, the nanny can provide the special care and attention needed by an infant.

Housewifery Help—Help with the children's laundry, the cleaning of bedrooms, playrooms, and children's bathrooms, and preparing and feeding children their evening meals are of great benefit to active parents. Most nannies provide this housewifery help on a daily basis.

Live-In Dependability—Because her commute is a mere twelve steps up the stairs, the live-in nanny is usually quite dependable. The typical causes of delay or absenteeism (rain, snow, traffic, etc...) are no excuse for the live-in, and consequently parents are able to leave the home at their intended time daily.

Bonding—While a child might feel warmth toward a teacher or day care mother, the relationship is rarely as close as with a nanny. The child is able to bond with a special surrogate parent, making the daily transition from parent to care provider easier.

THE CON'S

Caliber and Cost—The professional nanny is one of the most expensive forms of childcare—as expensive as a year of college at some very good schools. As one mother said, "I've got to sell a lot of computers to pay the cost of my childcare!" Naturally, cost is usually related to quality, with the highly qualified nannies demanding a top salary. Since there are so many more families seeking nannies than there are available applicants, most nannies find the highest market price is not difficult to command. Therefore, some very good families who are not able to be competitive in salary find themselves having to either lower their standards or choose another form of childcare.

Privacy—Lack of privacy is often the hardest adjustment for both the nanny and the family. Most families are not accustomed to having a stranger in the home. Likewise, the first-time live-in nanny is not used to living in someone else's home. To overcome this problem, many families

7

choose to either create very separate accommodations, or invite the nanny to become a member of the family.

Back-Up Help—While day care centers can still operate if one or two of their staff are out, the private home must have a backup system for the nanny who is ill, on vacation, or has an emergency of her own. This system is also essential in the unfortunate event that the nanny leaves without notice (not unheard of in this very personal work relationship). This backup help is often as difficult to find as was the nanny herself.

Lack of Supervision—The nanny has no direct supervision for the hours that her employers are out of the home. Many parents are uncomfortable with this situation, and resort to surprise visits to the home or frequent phone calls to check in on the household events. Others require that the nanny fill out a daily log (see page 107). However, once the relationship between the nanny and family is well established and trust develops, this concern usually fades.

Personal Involvement—The in-home relationship requires, indeed must be based on, a great deal of interpersonal communication. Nannies not only move in with clothes and knick-knacks, but personal habits, religious practices and a social life as well. Families must understand that the relationship will not be left solely to business issues. Some degree of personal involvement will be required to make the total relationship run smoothly, and many families feel this is an added burden to their already hectic lives.

Taxes—Like any other employer, the in-home employer must file for the employees social security, workman's compensation, and unemployment tax. These and other employer-required responsibilities can increase the total cost of a nanny almost 18% yearly (not including additional fees if an accountant does the work).

Types Of In-Home Childcare

I have found there are four general types of in-home childcare providers: the housekeeper/babysitter, the au pair, the college degreed nanny, and the trained nanny graduate. Each type has it's advantages and disadvantages.

THE HOUSEKEEPER/BABYSITTER

The Housekeeper/Babysitter provides all basic household help within a single salary. She will take care of the household chores in addition to providing basic childcare. She is usually foreign or part of the American lower-income bracket. Some housekeeper/babysitter types also are household managers, responsible for grocery shopping, arranging for household repairs, and for some families, even managing the household budget. Those who are household managers are few and far between, and as you might expect, cost a mint!

The basic housekeeper/babysitter has her advantages. For busy parents, one employee is easier to deal with than are several. The housekeeper/babysitter will usually cost less than the trained nanny. In addition, many families find there are less interpersonal conflicts than there would be with someone more highly trained. There are also drawbacks to this type of care provider. First, her educational limitations can prevent her from participating in the well-rounded upbringing of your child. Second, many of these providers are in the field because they are not qualified to do anything else, not because it is their first occupational choice. Third, if the care provider is a foreigner, language can be a barrier to a smooth running household. It can also prevent the newly speaking child from getting consistent support in the English language.

Lastly, if the housekeeper/babysitter is foreign and not legally permitted to work in the U.S., you may be required to sponsor her in order for her to work legally. (See page 20 for sponsoring information.)

THE AU PAIR

The Au Pair expects an exchange relationship. Usually an au pair is a younger girl, often from a European country or the midwest. She will exchange the experience of a new city and lifestyle, and a small amount of spending moncy, for either full or part-time childcare. She is usually considered a part of the family, not an employee. (Many families abuse this exchange, however, and the au pair becomes an overworked servant.)

The greatest benefit of this type of care provider is quality babysitting-style childcare for minimal cost. Drawbacks include employers feeling that this younger woman is more like another child in the family. In addition to going through the adjustment of relocation, she will go through the natural stages of growing up, and this can interfere with her job performance. While her English is usually at least understandable, proper grammar can be a problem. Finally, her childcare experience will probably be limited to babysitting and caring for siblings.

THE COLLEGE-DEGREED NANNY

The College-degreed Nanny is usually in her early to late twenties, with a two- or four-year degree in education, early child development, or a related field. Occasionally she is in her thirty's and taking a sabatical from a teaching profession or in her late fifties or sixties looking for a family to "retire" into. She has usually had substantial hands-on experience with children in various paid and volunteer positions. This nanny will probably only be interested in working for one to two years, using the experience as a stepping stone or resting place in her career.

This type of care provider has some important positive

aspects. She will be able to educate your child in the non-structured environment of the home. In addition, because of her similar cultural background, she can best bring the "extended family" concept to your childcare situation. But there are drawbacks as well. First, the college-degreed nanny has rarely had prior live-in nanny experience. Second, the in-home relationship is difficult to master with this type of person as she will expect to be treated like a professional, though entering a position with a traditional "servant" status. Finally, she will most likely be accepting of light housework responsibilities, but usually will expect there to be a housekeeper in the home at least once a week for heavy cleaning.

THE NANNY TRAINING GRADUATE

The Nanny Training Graduate will be one of two types. The nanny may be the traditionally-trained NNEB (those with the National Nanny Examination Board certificate) or a graduate of one of the new training programs now available in the United States. (It is important to note that these training programs are very new, and have yet to prove themselves over time. In addition there are no accreditation guidelines yet enforced. Therefore, subjects you might have assumed would be covered in training may not have been.) See suggestions under training schools in chapter 5.

Positive attributes to this type overlap with those of the college degreed nanny. In addition, she will usually have training more specific to the in-home position and a longer term interest in the nanny profession. As sought after as this type is, she also has some drawbacks. First, many families have found both the English and American trained nanny to be less flexible about added job responsibilities which do not involve the children than those who are not trained. Second, many American trained applicants are first-time nannies and are often only eighteen or nineteen years old. Finally, the European trained nanny can have more personal problems in adjusting to her new environment (much as the au pair would) if she has not previously worked in the U.S.

While the individual care provider can have characteristics of more than one of these categories, these are the basic groups. I know some college degreed nannies who do the housework for extra money. I also know trained nannies who's personal maturity level prevents them from truly holding the title of professional. In any event, in keeping with my definition of professional childcare, I refer generally to the last two types as those with the ability to perform as a professional nanny.

Why Nannying Is A Sound Professional Option

I have been asked many times by clients "Why would someone bright, caring, and educated want to work in my home?" (This is often said with a hint of distaste, as if childrearing were not something to be valued!) I am tempted to respond by saying "Don't look a gift horse in the mouth," but instead I explain a few, simple points:

1) Many women throughout the U.S. grow up with pride in housewifery and childcare skills. To these women, professionalism is not defined by wearing a business suit and carrying a briefcase, but by doing a job well, with integrity. Because they see the importance of quality childrearing, these women will feel pride in their nanny position.

2) Teaching jobs today, especially in the midwest, are scarce. The opportunity for a job with a good salary, free room and board, and many other benefits is very attractive. While this may not be a long term career goal, it can be a perfect one or two year stepping stone.

3) The nanny profession pays well. Most professional nannies who have been in the field for at least three years will earn salaries comparable to those of teachers, but with

all living expenses taken care of as well! Those using this profession as a stepping stone often find this position better enables them to save money for future endeavors or to pay back school loans than would the typical straight salaried job.

4) Young people can satisfy their desire for different experiences—new places, new people, new work challenges—through this opportunity. Older people can find financial security in a family setting, using some of their most overlooked skills.

Live-In vs. Live-Out

A professional nanny can either live in the home with her employers or live out of the employers home and come to the home daily. The decision to have a "live-in" or "live-out" usually depends on the needs, available space, and privacy preferences of the individual family. Sometimes however, the decision depends on what the best nanny applicant is looking for.

Below are listed some of the necessary considerations for families choosing between the live-in or live-out options.

Cost of Living and the Live-Out—Many families would prefer a live-out nanny. For the professional nanny, however, salary and cost of living are what will dictate the ability to live-out and still maintain a professional's salary. While $200.00 per week is a good salary if room, board, and other benefits are included, it is barely a living for the live-out, especially in a higher cost-of-living area. Because many families cannot afford $300 a week plus benefits for the professional live-out, it is common that the live-out is the less expensive housekeeper/babysitter type.

Space Requirements—Usually a private room and bath shared with a child is the minimum acceptable to the

13

live-in nanny. Increasing the attractiveness of the accommodations are: private bath, sitting room, private entrance, a refrigerator or kitchenette, or ultimately a full apartment. Spacious accommodations often outweigh an added $25.00 per week in salary when a nanny is deciding between two otherwise similar families.

Cost Differences—Cost differences will be substantial between a live-in and a live-out nanny of the same professional level. To be in the competitive market for a professional nanny, employers will need to use the following formula: a live-out will require the same base salary as the live-in, plus the cost of renting a small nearby apartment and a stipend for food and transportation.

Privacy Issues—Some families feel that a live-in would strictly limit their privacy. Families wary of this can choose one of two options. First, they can completely rule out live-in help, which may disqualify some very good candidates. Second, the family can arrange for a separate living area, perhaps with a private entrance and small kitchenette so that the nanny lives in, but is rarely in the common areas of the house when off duty. This investment will often increase the value of the home as well as make the position more attractive to prospective nannies. Also, a private apartment in a nearby neighborhood could be rented for the nanny.

Flexibility—Flexibility is one of the main issues families consider when deciding to have a live-in or live-out. Those applicants who live out often have families of their own, and they prefer to work eight hours a day as opposed to twelve. Most nannies who live in accept the ten to twelve hour day as the norm. Live-in nannies may also be more willing to accept evening or emergency care. While live-in nannies may charge for the extra hours, families are at least more certain about their flexibility and availability.

14

The Sliding Scale of Qualifications

Salaries for nannies, both live-in and live-out, depend greatly on such things as cost of living, added benefits, and job responsibilities. Of even stronger influence on salaries are the applicant's education level, prior experience, and personal attributes. The following checklist will help evaluate requirements and determine salary range. In general, if you have made many checks, you will be on the high end of the salary range for your community. If you have just a few checks you will be towards the lower end. (However, not all items to be checked are of equal value—i.e. a drivers license is easier to come by and less valuable than 4 years live-in experience. Therefore, you will have to take the value of a certain qualification into account to find your true position in the market.) Remember to weigh this checksheet with the following one on responsibilities.

Note: You may also use this as a checksheet of qualifications when interviewing candidates to see where they might be in the market!

CHECKSHEET OF REQUIRED QUALIFICATIONS

General

_____ Minimum (18) (20) (25) (35) (45) years of age
_____ Driver's license
_____ Correct use of English
_____ Ability to cook (basic) (well)

Educational

_____ Minimum H.S. Degree or equivalency
_____ Some college study
_____ Minimum (two-year) (four-year) degree
_____ Degree in (Education) (Early Childhood Education) (Pediatric Nursing) (Child

15

Development)   (any of the above)
_____ Special Education studies or degree

Specific Areas of Knowledge

_____ Basic nutrition for children
_____ Child-proofing a home
_____ Sanitation, including bottle sterilization
_____ Children's hygiene, including teaching good
practices to children
_____ Toilet training theories
_____ Sewing skills
_____ Swimming/water safety
_____ Etiquette and manners for children
_____ Family relationships and dynamics
_____ Identification of emotional problems with children
_____ Child observation skills
_____ Development of children's play activities
_____ Creative reading to children
_____ CPR for children
_____ Basic and emergency first aid
_____ Teaching arts and crafts
_____ Recreation leadership skills
_____ Professional roles, attitudes, and
behaviors within the individual family

Personal

_____ Ability to commit for a minimum of   (one)   (two)
year(s)
_____ Good health, including non-obesity
_____ Single, with no dependants (if live-in)
_____ Minimum three personal references from those
who have known applicant for at least 2 years
_____ Effective communication skills
_____ Willingness to travel

Personality

_____ Effective rapport builder with children

_____ Flexible nature
_____ Creative talents
_____ Empathetic/compassionate nature
_____ Professional attitude

Experience, With References To Verify:
_____ Care of own children
_____ Minimum 2 years of any type experience with children
_____ Minimum 2 years part time paid care of children
_____ Minimum 2 years full time paid care of children
_____ Minimum 1 year full time nanny experience
_____ More than 1 year full time nanny experience
_____ Care of sick children
_____ Care of infants/toddlers
_____ Care of older children/teenagers
_____ Care of the exceptional child
_____ Home management experience

The Sliding Scale of Job Descriptions

Like salaries, job responsibilities vary from family to family. While it is commonly agreed that professional childcare providers are not responsible for more than light housework, individual nannies will differ in attitude toward specific added responsibilities. Below is a guideline for families who use Nanny Placement Services, Inc. We have listed first what we feel to be the responsibilities of *any* in-home childcare provider. Second, we list a checksheet of negotiable responsibilities. It is important for families to realize that while these additional responsibilities are considered negotiable, they may take a family out of the market for the professional nanny. Of course, salary must also increase with the amount of responsibilities required. Once both checksheets are completed, weigh them together. For example, if your qualifications are at a high level but your additional responsibilities are minimal (or vice versa) then you are probably in a middle salary range.

ALL NANNIES ARE EXPECTED TO CHEERFULLY:

1) Provide childcare up to 12 hours per day, five consecutive days per week.

2) Provide "light housewifery," which includes doing children's laundry, cleaning the children's bedrooms, playrooms and bathrooms, preparing and cleaning up from children's snacks and meals, and doing child-related errands.

3) Plan nutritious meals and snacks for children.

4) Use creative skills to plan activities that promote the physical, emotional, intellectual, and social development of the child.

5) Comply with parents' mode of discipline and child-rearing preferences.

6) Demonstrate a helpful attitude while on duty.

7) Promote feelings of security and warmth; plan cuddle/read/talk time daily with child.

8) Record daily log sheets of events and confer daily with parents about special problems, child's newly learned skills, etc. so as to promote good communication with parent's concerning child's daytime life.

9) Provide **reasonable** flexibility in times of parent's emergency or unexpected schedule changes.

10) Read/review any professionally-related materials provided by parents to promote broader knowledge of child-rearing philosophy, education, and child psychology.

11) Actively participate in understanding special problems or interests the children may have, providing possible solutions for the former, and activities to promote the latter.

12) Provide an optimum learning situation for the child by communication with school teachers and coordinating home learning time with school learning time.

CHECKSHEET FOR ADDITIONALLY REQUIRED RESPONSIBILITIES

_____ Full family meal preparation
_____ Full family laundry
_____ Full family ironing
_____ Family grocery shopping
_____ Family errands
_____ Daily household tidying after parents
_____ Bed-making for entire family
_____ Household vacuuming, dusting, cleaning of baths
_____ Daily cleanup after family meals
_____ Overtime/evening care over normally sheduled hours
_____ Less than two consecutive full days off
_____ Family entertaining tasks (serving, preparation work)
_____ Occasional 24 hour care
_____ Frequent 24 hour care
_____ Periodic heavy cleaning (cleaning stove and refrigerator, polishing silver, organizing family closets, etc.)
_____ Home management (supervision of other staff, bookkeeping, arranging for household repair, etc.)
_____ Other _____
_____

Sponsoring The Foreign Nanny
—Miriam Freilicher, Attorney at Law

If your nanny is not a United States citizen, she must obtain a permanent resident visa—the "green card"—to live permanently in the U.S. with permission to work. Under present Federal Law, there are no employer penalties for hiring workers who do not have "green cards." Some State laws, however, do provide sanctions for employers that hire aliens who do not have work permission. You should check with your State Attorney General's office to find out if there are employer sanctions in your state.

There are basically two ways to obtain permanent residence status: 1) through sponsorship by a close relative who is a U.S. Citizen or permanent resident; and 2) through a petition based on a job offer and sponsorship by an employer. If an alien can qualify as a refugee and apply for asylum status that may also, in a few cases, lead to permanent residence.

If you as an employer sponsor your nanny for permanent residence, you must show that she will not be taking a job from a U.S. worker. Any employer's application for labor certification is complicated. You must prove to the Department of Labor through newspaper advertising that qualified U.S. workers are not available. You will probably need the help of an attorney specializing in immigration law. Once labor certification is granted and your nanny meets all other immigration requirements, permanent residence status is granted.

Employer petitions may be filed for classification under what are called either the third or sixth preference categories. The third preference is for those workers who hold at least a bachelor's degree (or equivalent), and who will be working in a position that requires at least a bachelor's degree. The sixth preference is for all other workers whose skills and services are needed by an employer and who will not be taking a job from a U.S. worker. It is necessary to wait longer for a completed visa under the sixth preference due to demand for visas in that category. A third preference application could take as long as one year, while a sixth preference is likely to take about two years to complete.

Many positions held by nannies in the U.S. can qualify for labor certification approval which is a prerequisite to obtaining permanent resident status. The petition for permanent residence status is filed with the Immigration and Nationalization Service. Upon approval of the petition, the nanny can change her status to that of permanent resident through adjustment of status procedures in the U.S. (if she is in the U.S. and has no authorized employment) or through visa processing abroad at the U.S. Consulate in her home country.

The first step for those seeking to sponsor a nanny is to contact an immigration attorney for advice. From there, an employer can choose to work on their own, (however sponsoring is very complicated and procedures must be followed carefully). Most employers choose to hire the immigration attorney to handle these procedures. The cost for these services may vary, depending primarily on the rates for legal services in your community, and of course, the experience and reputation of the attorney. In a large metropolitan area, sponsoring will cost anywhere from $1,500.00 up to several thousand dollars.

Miriam Freilicher is an Attorney at Law, specializing in immigration law. Her practice is based in Washington, D.C.

CHAPTER 2

FINDING QUALIFIED NANNY APPLICANTS

One day a client walked into my office, weary from the summer heat and her pregnancy, and begged for help. She compared nanny-hunting to panning for gold in the California gold rush days. Everyone, she was sure, who had found a competent, loving, and experienced nanny had either "begged, borrowed or stolen." Sighing that she had tried the latter two to no avail, she was ready to beg.

While agencies, nanny schools, and word-of-mouth are possible sources for locating applicants, there are no guarantees. As in a gold rush, many people are searching for the same precious commodity, and their efforts are rewarded only after much "digging and sifting." My client, it turned out, had to wait another month before she found the right person—only three short weeks before the end of her maternity leave.

Listed below are several avenues for finding applicants. Because the pool of applicants is limited, I suggest that the private family use as many of the following recruitment options as possible. Even by using all options, most families will probably have very few *quality* candidates to review for their nanny position.

Local Newspapers

Placing ads in local newspapers is the first route most people use to seek out qualified applicants. In major cities however, due to the overwhelming number of unqualified applicants who respond, this method can be a long and frustrating one. While most nannies do read the papers, they too become frustrated with the difficulty in finding a good family among the mass of ads. It is easier for them to either use an agency, which will have already screened families for vital information, or listen for good openings through the nanny grapevine.

It is possible to find someone good using a newspaper, but only with a great deal of perserverance. To start off on the right foot, write an ad which stands out from the rest in the paper you use. I offer the following suggestions for writing an ad:

1) Don't be cheap. The longer your ad, the more likely it is to be read. By explaining your situation in detail you will eliminate many of the calls which would waste your time.

2) Don't ask for resumes through the mail. It automatically makes the hiring process too long for both you and the applicant. Remember, there are many families out there who can be called immediately. Applicants will in all probability have accepted a job by the time you have reviewed the resume, if anyone has bothered to send one at all.

3) Don't emphasize how sweet, adorable, or cute your child is, thus appearing biased to a fault. If you want to show warmth or personality in your ad, use words such as "happy" or "energetic" (if applicable) when describing your child or children. Better still, you might describe the family as a whole, using adjectives which will let some of your family personality show.

4) Do include your location, accessability to public trans-

portation, number and ages of children, starting salary range, and hours.

5)   Do include any perks or benefits you can think of! You need to "sell" your job and family. Such perks might include pool priveleges, employees portion of Social Security taxes paid, use of private car, travel, or extensive vacation time.

6)   Do make your requirements known. If good English is a must, put it in bold letters. (You reduce yor risk of non-English speaking applicants calling if "**ENGLISH**" is emphasized.) Other requirements should be made known as well, but only list the absolutes. If you want to list a requirement that is not an absolute, use the word "Prefer." Be certain to list your requirements last. Sell them first, then weed them out.

7)   Plan to run your ad a minimum of two Sundays, adding Saturday for best results. Mid-week is also success-ful in most papers if the ad is run at least three days consecutively.

With all this in mind, a good ad might read as follows:

> "**NANNY NEEDED** live-out, M—F, 8:00-6:30, in Home-town for two girls ages 13 months and 3 years. These happy children and their parents offer use of family pool, $225 p/w, health insurance after 3 months and two weeks paid vacation yearly. **REQUIREMENTS** include top **ENGLISH** skills, minimum 1 year childcare expe-rience, non-smoker, prefer a driver with own car. Call early eves/wknds to John or Mary at (301) 555-1212."

Out-Of-Town Newspapers

Many families seeking live-in nannies will be successfull using out-of-town newspaper ads. Travel and striking out on one's own has long held excitement for young, crea-tive, and adventurous spirits. At the same time, older individuals who no longer have families at home can become a "grand-nanny." What you offer to those in other parts of the country is an opportunity. Your job will be to distinguish the "easy opportunity" seekers from those who will enjoy and appreciate the job *as a job*. (See chapter three for information on screening applicants.)

Deciding where to place the ad depends on what is most convenient for you. Many families feel that the midwest yields the greatest amount of quality applicants. If you have friends or relatives in another part of the U.S., ask them about their local papers, and if they would consider interviewing a prospective nanny for you once you have narrowed your choices down to one or two.

Another option may be to interview in the area you will be traveling to on business. By spending an extra day interviewing, you cut costs and meet prospective nannies in person.

To place an ad in another city, call the paper you are interested in and ask for the out-of-state classified department. Usually you will have to pay for the ad before it appears, so plan to call at least 10 days before you want the ad to run. You may also have to pay an out-of-state rate for advertising, which can be substantially higher than the local rate. If you have a friend or relative in that area, have them place it for you at the local rate to minimize the cost.

Agencies

As interest in the American nanny increases, placement agencies are beginning to flourish even more so than training schools. While not all have excellent reputations, there are far too many which do to list. This is primarily due to the fact that many agencies are one woman operations. These women act as liaisons and can often be quite helpful. Other agencies have a full staff, written policies, and are well advertised. When choosing an agency (and I suggest using as many as you feel are reputable) it is important to find out the following things:

1) What is the agency's reputation in your community? Have friends used them? If so, was a successful placement the result of luck, or did the agency offer several viable possibilities? Does the agency belong to the Better Business Bureau? If not, you may be able to check on them by contacting past clients. Of course, any past clients the agency lets you contact will have favorable reports. (If an agency refuses to pass out references, they may simply be protecting their clients' privacy, not their own poor performance.)

2) What is the agency's acceptance criteria? Do they consider education, experience, references, or all of these? Do they have a minimum age requirement? Must their nannies be U.S. Citizens? If not, are your expected to sponsor the nanny—and is the agency operating legally?

3) What are the agency's reference checking policies? Do they allow old references (babysitting references from 5 years before), references from relatives, or written references from those you cannot contact personally? How many references do they require, and how many have to be within the childcare field? Do they check the nanny's last place of employment, no matter what kind of job it was? Do they require a complete work history, or only babysitting references of neighbors? *Are you allowed to recheck?* (I feel this last point is essential to your own peace of mind. Since families approached directly by other families are often more open in their evaluations, you may even learn more than the agency did.)

4) What is their interview process? Do they have a personal interveiw with the applicant prior to accepting them? Are you allowed a screening phone conversation before meeting the applicant? Must you hire sight unseen?

5)   What are the agencies fees and refund policies? (If you must hire sight unseen, there should be a 100% refund for at least the first week.) Many agencies will have a sliding scale for refund, depending on how long you have the nanny, while others have a flat rate for a certain period of time. Explore also whether the nanny is charged a fee, and what her refund rights are regarding an unsuccessful placement. Most agencies will expect payment after verbal commitment to hire, but before the nanny begins. Find out what happens if you don't pay on time.

6)   Does the agency require that you sign a contract? If so, read the contract thoroughly. Be certain it does not require you to pay a fee to them if you find a nanny somewhere else.

7)   Do they offer support services for both the nanny and the family after placement, such as liaison services between family and nanny or information at tax time, etc.?

It is a general rule of thumb that if the agency has very high quality applicants, their fee will be higher. It is inexpensive to refer domestic help, but very costly to recruit educated professionals. If in the end the candidate is good, but not good enough to justify the fee, don't hire her. If she is, assume it is part of your expenses in recruiting a professional.

Nanny Training Courses

Nanny training schools and programs are listed in chapter 5. When trying to recruit from these schools, it is important to remember that not all schools are alike. At this time, there is no national accreditation system. I suggest the following guidelines when working with an institution of training for placement:

1)   Know what you can expect. What are their entrance requirements? What is their general curriculum, and how in-depth is each subject covered? How successfully must the nanny pass each subject to be certified?

2)   Before traveling to an institution far away, ask how many nannies are coming available, and what are the procedures for interviewing. Also ask about the number of other families flying out to see the same graduates.

3)   After giving the details of your position, ask if you are offering the same salary and have the same expectations as other recruiting families. If you are not in the individual school's competitive market you will be wasting your time trying to recruit through them.

4)   Ask if there is a fee. Many schools have their own placement centers and will charge you as an agency would. As with an agency, be sure to review your contract with the placement center carefully. Many schools require that their graduate nannies and hiring families contract together as well. It is important to be aware of these procedures and policies.

5)   Remember that if the school has a good reputation and a fair amount of publicity, you will be one of *many* families calling with the same questions. Be polite, and be sure the time you take is as short as possible. Most training directors wear several hats in the organization, and their time is valuable and limited. Make it as convenient as possible for them and they will be more willing to be as helpful to you as possible.

The Infamous "Word-Of-Mouth"

Before there were quality agencies and American training schools, most families relied upon word-of-mouth to find nanny applicants. Today, many families still swear by it for finding the best applicants in the shortest amount of time.

Word-of-mouth, for those new to the nanny world, is a form of recruiting which is really just telling *everyone* and *anyone* who might know of an unhappy, unemployed, or soon-to-be unemployed nanny that you are in the market for a nanny. Quality and experienced nannies are snatched up faster than bad news travels. It is your lucky day if your name is on the grapevine when a good one announces her availability.

Word-of-mouth, I have found, works best with families who know many other families who employ nannies. For the executive female with primarily male professional associates, word-of-mouth may not take her too far. However, networking, very similar to word-of-mouth, is available to all in need of nannies.

Begin your networking by contacting your local church or synagogue. Ask about any of their members who may be in need of employment, including active "grandmother types" who are perhaps widowed and struggling. Ask your friends across the country to do the same. Visit your local day care center and ask around (quietly, I suggest) if anyone there might be interested in a one-on-one child-care situation. Day care teachers and assistants are usually overworked, underpaid, and have a high rate of burnout. Call your local college employment service for graduates or students who may want to take a year off their studies. Put up signs at the grocery store, drug store, and advertise in community newspapers. Try every option you can think of.

How Long Will It Take?

Finding the right nanny can take a few days or several months. If your position is attractive, your *exact* starting date flexible, and you are very actively recruiting, I feel a good nanny can be found in 3-5 weeks. It is difficult to find the applicant of your dreams on one week's notice but I have seen it happen. Likewise, few applicants are willing to wait around 3 months for the position to start, but I have seen that happen too. For best results, start about 8 weeks before you know you will need someone.

CHAPTER 3

SCREENING APPLICANTS

O nce a possible applicant has been located, an unbiased and *non-desperate* screening process must begin. Many families have made mistakes with other applicants in the past, and therefore no longer trust their own judgement. Others interviewing for the first time do not know what questions to ask, how to reference check, or how and when to offer the position.

The most important thing to remember when screening a seemingly good applicant is not to wear rose colored glasses. Just because a nanny has written references in hand and a winning personality there is no excuse for poor screening. (Some nannies with many bad references, a history of drug or alcohol use, or an unstable personality can continue to get jobs because prospective employers like her enough and are weary enough of the whole recruiting process that they don't reference check.)

The following information is for every family who hires a nanny, whether they use an agency, newspaper advertising, or hear of someone by word of mouth. Remember that much of what makes a good nanny comes from her personality. When both interviewing and reference checking families must be prepared to do a lot of listening, reading between the lines, and personality assessing.

Telephone Interviewing

All applicants, whether local or not, should be contacted by phone. This method both eliminates those obviously unqualified and gives a basic feel for the applicant before she enters your home. I offer the following suggestions for telephone interviewing:

1) When interviewing, have a list of qualities and abilities that you are looking for. You may want to photocopy this list, so you can make comments during each applicant's phone call. On the list, have three catagories: Essential, Preferred, and Other Bonuses. Under each category, list items such as swimming ability, non-smoker, driver, top English and grammar skills, long term commitment, education, live-in experience, etc. Be sure to include anything and everything that could influence your decision.

2) Also have a list of your requirements and job description, and give this information over the phone. Detail salary range, accommodations, hours, days off, vacation or other benefits, and let the prospective nanny know if any of these requirements are negotiable.

3) To ensure that the applicant is, at this point, still interested, tell her to think about the information you have given, and then to call you back to schedule an interview. Some people feel pressured to interview even if they don't like the position you have described. You would be surprised how many appear to be taking directions to your home, never intending to show up.

4) If they do call back, you can be sure they are interested. Set up a time for a personal interview, preferably in your home, that is convenient to both of you. Set a specific time, but ask them to call you just before they leave. This way they can be sure you know any delays were caused by unfamiliarity with area, traffic problems, etc. and not by a possible chronic punctuality problem.

5) Even if an agency sets up an interview, insist on talking to the candidate yourself first. Many agencies pay little attention to your requirements, and send a completely inappropriate person. (If this happens more than once, stop dealing with the agency.)

Personal Interviewing

By the time you are ready to conduct the personal interview, you should know the applicant's basic qualifications. You will now conduct a "fine tuning" interview, assessing such things as motivation, personality, hands-on ability with your child, and personal habits. The following suggestions will help you make the most of this interview:

1) Have your children around for the first part of the interview, but arrange for them to be away while you talk business. This first lets you see how the applicant and your children respond to each other and then allows you the ability to talk without interruption.

2) Observe the applicant for personal idiosyncrasies, good hygiene, tasteful and appropriate dress, politeness, and other characteristics important to your family. Note anything you wish to discuss with your spouse after the interview.

3) Recheck the list you went over on the phone. Restate your expectations and job description, and then in relation to what you know of the applicant, let her know the salary you would be willing to offer if you indeed do hire her.

4) Introduce your former nanny (if there is one), and allow the two to meet alone for a short period of time. The applicant can then do a "reference check" on you. Families who do not provide this interview because of an

unhappy relationship are not being fair. After all, you should expect a nanny with an unhappy relationship to provide that reference just the same.

5)   Make up a list of "what if" questions for the nanny to answer. For example, "What if Jamie, (who is two), is having a temper tantrum because we are leaving for work early and don't have time to feed him his breakfast as usual?" Try not to sound like a quizmaster, but instead someone interested in nanny's childrearing and discipline philosophies. Don't argue a "wrong answer," but let her know how you would respond, and ask her if she would be willing to respond according to your directed methods.

6)   Let her know if she is being considered for your position if indeed she is. An apathetic "we'll call you" after an interview can make her feel she did not interview well. She may take another offer because she does not feel your's will come through.

7)   Do not make an offer until you have thoroughly checked her references. Even if an agency claims they check references, you should check them again yourself, to your own satisfaction. Prior to your own check, you should ask the agency to read you or show you the reference checking information they have received to better prepare yourself for your call to the reference.

8)   Like the telephone interview, it is best to ask the applicant to call you in one or two days if she is interested in the job. However, she may be under the time constraints of another offer. In this case, you will have to work within her time frame if you decide you would like to hire her.

9)   Many families choose to hold a secondary interview by observing the prospective nanny at work in their home. While the trial period can run anywhere from one day to two weeks, it is customary for the family to offer compensation for this time. Most families agree that for the stability

of the children they will only "trial run" very promising candidates. Likewise, applicants don't want to waste the time they could be spending job hunting unless the job looks promising to them as well.

Reference Checking

Reference checking is an art, and one to be taken seriously. Use the following suggestions and the reference checking form on the next pages when checking references.

Require at least three references. At least two of them should come from employers who have observed the applicant in a child-related position. The third reference may verify the applicant's other employment, academic, or personal accomplishments. Be sure to check the applicant's latest work reference, no matter what type of work it is.

Require phone numbers, not just addresses, and double check all written references. Written references with no way to contact the writer are not valid.

When calling a reference, start off by introducing yourself and why you are calling, mentioning that the applicant *Jane Doe* had given you her number. Ask for 10 minutes of their time. If you sense that it is not the best time for them to talk, offer to call back at the reference givers convenience. You want them to give you detailed information, and those who are in a hurry or are otherwise occupied will most likely be too brief.

1)   Reassure the reference giver that whatever you hear will be kept in the strictest confidence, and the applicant need not even know that you were able to contact them if they prefer. This is the only way a family who fears repercussions of a bad reference will open up to you. (If you make this promise—keep it!)

2) If the person you are calling has provided the applicant with a written reference, let them know you are verifying it and tell them to feel free to repeat themselves. Often the tone of voice will tell you more than the written word.

3) Ask several open-ended questions of which you already know the answers. For example, the applicant may have said she worked for 2 years and was paid $175 per week. Ask the reference "How long did she work for you, and what was her salary?" This way you can check the validity of the applicant's reference. If you question the reference's validity, be sure to ask more open-ended questions.

4) Explain to the reference giver the nature of the position. Let the reference giver know that you need to understand the applicant's personality, including both strengths and weaknesses, in order to feel comfortable about hiring her. Also mention that in order for the applicant to be happy, she must also be able to handle certain strengths and weaknesses in your family. Explain your lifestyle as best you can, and ask if they feel the applicant would be happy in your home. What potential problems do they feel could arise?

5) While most references will not lie, some will not mention problem areas unless specifically asked. Any time that you feel you hear some hesitation, zoom in on it. You might say "I hear some hesitation in your voice, was there some questionable incident or other reason for that hesitation?"

6) Remember in the case of a bad reference that the employer is not always right. One way to tell an unfair reference is by listening for the level of anxiety in the reference giver's voice. If there were no specific incidences mentioned, but the tone was tense and the overall reference was bad, it may have been a personality conflict. Not all employers are easy to work for, especially in the

in-home relationship. You will have to use your own judgement by comparing what several references say.

Hiring "Sight Unseen"

A trial run for at least two weeks is essential for those hiring "sight unseen" from another part of the country. This trial run gives both parties a chance to get to know each other before a commitment is made. I offer these suggestions to those hiring "sight unseen":

1) Check all references first. The applicant may be a dream over the phone, but without reference checking you may find out too late that she has a history of job hopping or some other undesirable trait.

2) Ask for a written resume. This gives you both a feel for her organization of thoughts and a full background on experience and education.

3) If she is young, talk to her parents or other relatives. Find out if she will be supported in the move, and if they feel she can handle it. Parental support is a must when homesickness and readjustment problems inevitably set in during the first few weeks! (One self-determined young woman I know felt the move would be a way to "show them all" that she could do it. In the end, she couldn't—as her family who knew her well had expected.)

4) Offer to pay for her transportation for a trial 2 weeks of work, but let her know that she will be compensating for half of that cost through a deduction from her salary. Requiring that the nanny make an investment in the trial run will eliminate the candidate merely looking for a free trip.

5) Remember that you may decide not to hire her even before the two weeks are up. If you choose not to finish out the time, you will not receive work for her half of the transportation costs. This you must consider your loss as the result of a risk taken.

39

Background Checks and Pyschological Assessments
—Judith Bunge, Ph.D.

Families who consider hiring a nanny are justifiably concerned with the background and history of each individual they consider. The nanny is intimately involved with the family and this sensitive, important relationship must be based on trust and honesty. In addition to references and personal interviews, there are three more important steps which can be taken to assess an applicant's background. They are a check of police records, credit records and psychological assessments. Families will find that some nanny referrals provide information in all these areas, while others leave this responsibility up to the client family. The following information is provided to help families in assessing the information provided on each applicant, as well as tips which may help those who do these checks themselves.

Police and Credit Background Checks

If these data are gathered by the family, a permission waiver is first signed by the applicant. Police and credit checks vary widely in scope and cost.

A local records check can be requested by the applicant him/herself, usually at no cost. It can be completed by a private agency for a fairly low cost. Juvenile records cannot be opened.

A national records check can be accomplished in four basic ways. Credit checks are completed by credit information firms who charge approximately $30-40 as an initial fee and $2-3 per client. Police officers often conduct national police checks and charge at their regular private-duty rate, typically $15 or less per client. Private investigator charges typically start at $40 and may cost $100 or more, depending on the depth of the investigation. A police record search using fingerprints and including FBI information is the most expensive and extensive check. Costs depend on the charges of the person or agency doing the search.

Psychological Assessments

Psychological information also varies widely in type and scope. Two important points need to be mentioned. First, be sure that any personality or psychological test has been administered and scored by a professional and under valid testing conditions. Second and most important, all psychological/personality test data should be considered as one more piece of information about a client, not an infallible source of truth. Test data are guidelines to help a family assess an applicant, as is all other information pertaining to that person.

A wide variety of tests can be used, but examples of commonly used

40

instruments are:

The California Psychological Inventory is 35 minutes to 1 hour test requiring average reading skills. Administration and scoring does not need to be done by a psychologist.

The Minnesota Multiphasic Personality Inventory (MMPI) is a 2 hour test requiring average reading skills. It must be administered and scored by a psychologist trained for this test.

To inquire about other tests, ask your local mental health center.

The ultimate responsibility for assessing the suitability of a nanny applicant must rest with the family, but police checks, credit checks and psychological assessments can be valuable tools in the decision-making process.

Judith Bunge has her Ph.D. in Child Development, and is founder and executive director of North American Nannies Inc., a nanny training and placement school in Columbus, Ohio.

REFERENCE CHECKING FORM

Reference given by _____ Phone _____

Reference Check for _____ Date _____

Relation to applicant _____ Known for ____ years

Employment dates _____ to _____ Salary _____

Job Responsibilities _____

Reason for Leaving _____

ATTENDANCE:

Hardly ever missed work ____

No more than 8 days missed ____

10-12 days per year missed ____

Frequent absences, unreliable ____

PUNCTUALITY:

Never late ____

A few minutes late once a month ____

A half hour or less late per week ____

Late almost every day ____

OVERTIME:

Has worked overtime frequently/willingly ____

Occasional overtime with good attitude ____

Dislikes working overtime ____

Never ____

WORK QUALITY:

Top rate, very interested ____

Average, as expected ____

Occasionally below par ____

Often below expectations ____

ENGLISH SKILLS:

Verbal expression:	EXCELLENT	GOOD	FAIR	POOR
Writing skills:	EXCELLENT	GOOD	FAIR	POOR
Proper grammer usage:	EXCELLENT	GOOD	FAIR	POOR

Did the applicant actively participate in the education of the child (i.e. read books, play games, plan activities)?

ALWAYS   OFTEN   WHEN REQUESTED   SOMETIMES   NEVER

Please give examples _____

_____

Would the applicant need further training? _____

Drugs or alcohol use? _____ Excessive work leave? _____

Could and did applicant work effectively in the following situations: (Please give examples if possible)

Pressure/Emergency _____

A difficult family situation _____

Minimum supervision _____

With parent or supervisor in home _____

With other household staff/ teamwork _____

PERSONAL RELATIONS:
Loving with children? _____

Appropriate with employers? _____

Prone to personality conflicts? _____

Moody, irritable, or stubborn? _____

PERSONAL APPEARANCE/HYGIENE:
Always well-groomed   ____

Acceptable/casual appearance   ____

Poor appearance   ____

Serious appearance problems   ____

CRITICISM:
Able to accept and learn from it _____

Personally hurt if critisized _____

Takes offense _____

COMMENTS: _____

_____

_____

CHAPTER 4

YEARLY COST ANALYSIS

How much does a nanny *really* cost? Even families who employ nannies might not be able to tell you. There are a number of "hidden" costs involved. Many who hire a nanny at $200.00 per week expect a nanny to cost $10,400 per year. They are often disappointed when, after adding up the costs of recruitment, taxes, room and board, and all the "extras" needed to be competitive in the market, they realize that they have spend $14-18,000 in one year. Use the following guide to find average costs, and the following worksheet to determine your family's estimated yearly costs.

Recruitment Costs

Advertising in the want ads can run from $7-$125, depending on the length of the ad and the circulation of the paper. Advertising in out of town papers may cost you non-local rates, which can be substantially higher. Expect to run the ad several weeks in a row, and be thankful if one or two weeks is enough.

Agencies fees range from two weeks of the nanny's pay to 12% of the nanny's total yearly salary. Most agencies have no charge, or charge only a nominal fee for application. These services will only bill you if you hire one of their applicants.

Turnover is high in any form of childcare, including nannying. It is best to budget for two times the amount you expect for recruiting costs just in case. (Some families use this extra amount for a bonus at the end of the commitment term for the nanny who has stayed to the agreed date.)

Benefits

Benefits may include such things as health insurance, car for private use or paid car insurance premiums, two or more weeks paid vacation, national or international travel, completely separate or unusually attractive accommodations, memberships to family clubs or sports facilities, and provision of special dietary foods. Some benefits will cost more than others, and some cost nothing at all (i.e. use of family swimming pool). However, keep in mind the following about benefits:

1) Partial reimbursement for car insurance and gas allowances are not benefits if the nanny's car is being used for work related duties.

2) A minimum one week vacation is standard. It is usually taken at the end of the first year, or sometime during the first year at the family's convenience.

3) Travel is only a benefit if the nanny has the same amount of time off that she has when working at home and is provided with avenues to activities which are of interest to her during her free time.

4) At minimum, the live-in nanny must have a private room and shared bath. Accommodations become "benefits" if she has more than the minimum.

5) Board is included in the live-in situation. Special dietary desires are those foods you would not normally have in the household, but provide at the nannies special

request. Many families limit this in dollar amounts such as $15.00 per week.

Bonuses and Raises

Raises are often given every six months. A quality raise is 5-7% of her weekly salary. However, many families choose to give bonuses instead of raises. Bonuses are an effective way of showing appreciation for a nanny without raising her salary every 6 months. A bonus can be in the form of extra days off, transportation home at Christmas, cash, or other unique plans. Many families choose to give bonuses when nannies are performing exceptionally well, while others use it as a pick-me-up in bad or overly hectic times. In addition, a cost of living adjustment in salary should be made yearly as in any other job.

Back Up Care Costs

There will be times in the year when you will have to temporarily replace the nanny. If your back up system is a day care center, or a temporary nanny placement service, this will be an added cost. (Or if the back up person is you, you may be losing your own earnings.) In any case, this added cost is on top of the nannies usual salary (few families dock pay for up to 5 sick days). Estimate 8 days of the cost of your back-up system for nannies sick leave and emergency personal days. If your nanny takes her vacation at a different time than you do, you will have to budget for those added days too.

Room and Board

While a family might like to include room and board in the salary, it is against the law, But even if you have no additional construction or decorating expenses, such things as electricity, gas, water, and food consumption for the household do add up. Assume the nanny uses one adult portion of these expenses.

Health Insurance

Private insurance for individuals is extremely expensive. Group plans such as that offered by the National Association For The Education of Young Children can be relatively inexpensive. Many families offer health as a benefit after 3 or 6 months, in which case the quarterly cost would occur less often than four times during the first year.

Overtime Care

Most nannies expect a pay increase of time and a half for overtime care, such as twenty-four hour care while parents travel or additional evenings per week not contracted for. Estimate the amount of time you expect such events and multiply the time by one and a half of the regular salary (i.e., $200 per week=$40 per day, so 24 hours care on a normal working day would be $60.00).

Taxes

The law requires that both employers and employees pay taxes in the in-home childcare situation. Some families prefer to pay cash "under the table," however more and more families are getting caught as in-home childcare becomes popular, and the penalties are high. Understanding your requirements is not as difficult as you might think. A full, up to date package of information, forms, and examples can be obtained by writing the IRS and asking for the publication entitle *Child And Disabled Dependent Care*. Each state has individual requirements which can be obtained through your state tax agency. *(NOTE: Only cash paid is taxable, not benefit or room and board.)*

Federally Required—For Families

Social security is required when wages exceed $50 per calendar quarter. Employers pay a minimum of 7%, and employee 6.7% to be deducted from the employees wages and filed by the employer. The forms used by the IRS 942 and the W-2. The IRS 942 must be filed quarterly, the W-2 annually. The fine of non-compliance is 5% of the money owed per month, up to 25%. Interest charged for this money owed is 11% per year.

Unemployment tax is required when wages exceed $1,000 in any calendar quarter. The rate is 3.5% of the first $7,000, however state unemployment tax may also be charged and can be deducted up to 2.7%, depending on the individual state rate. The form to use is the IRS-940, filed annually. The non-compliance fine is the same as that for non-compliance of social security taxes. These taxes are the responsibility of the client and fines are charged to the employer.

Federally Required—For Nannies

Employee federal and state taxes are the responsibility of the employee. All employers are required to fill out and file the employees W-2 forms. However, it is not the responsibility of the employer to actually withhold the tax.

In-home childcare providers can either have their taxes withheld and file their taxes annually or be listed as a private contractor and file themselves quarterly. If employers do withhold however, they are legally required to pay the government at the end of the year the amount which was deducted. To file individually send for the information listed above.

TOTAL YEARLY COST WORKSHEET

Recruitment Expenses (x 2)   _____

Salary (weekly x 52)   _____

Taxes (Federal)   _____

Taxes (state)   _____

Health Insurance (Quarterly x __)   _____

Backup care costs   _____

Room and Board (monthly x 12)   _____

Overtime Care (monthly estimate x 12)   _____

Bonuses/Raises/Incentives   _____

TOTAL   _____

CHAPTER 5

TRAINING THE AMERICAN NANNY

Families paying the high costs of a qualified in-home nanny naturally want the best person they can find. This may mean hiring a nanny training school graduate, or creating an individual training program for a nanny already in the home. American nanny training schools have become very popular. New training sites have been springing up all over the country, in both the public and private sectors. However, because the American nanny is such a new phenomenon, many schools are able to recruit only a limited number of students each session. The number of graduates to date doesn't begin to approach the number of families contacting the schools with job offers.

Below are listed several of the currently operating nanny training schools.[1]

[1]. The American Council of Nanny Schools is an independently operated accrediting association; however is not yet recognized by the public sector. It was formed because there is no accrediting institution in the public or private sectors for the accreditation of nanny schools, yet a great need for one. The following is their mission statement:

"The American Council of Nanny Schools is a nonprofit coalition of accredited nanny schools seeking to educate, standardize, and promote the professional status of nannies in this country through accrediting new schools, providing professional support, and developing and administering a national competency test."

Those interested in more information about the council can contact Chairman Joy Shelton, Delta College, University Center, MI, 49710, (517) 686-9417.

Some are short term, intensive training, while others are longer term, offering college credits and even associate degrees. It is important for anyone interested in attending or recruiting from these schools to understand that there are no official standards or accreditation required for nanny training at this time. Therefore, do not assume a training school produces high quality care providers just because it offers a fancy brochure.

Before selecting a training program, check for the credentials of the educators and administrators. Ask many questions about the school's philosophy concerning the nanny profession, the amount and type of successful work needed to graduate, and the level of course difficulty. Ask about courses that cover the in-home relationship, family dynamics, and social etiquette. Take note of hands-on experiencial learning, and find out if *both* practical learning and child development theory are emphasized. Whether you are seeking training or are offering a job to a graduate, it is best to use the school which most closely identifies with your philosophy of professional in-home childcare.

American Nanny Plan, Inc.
P.O. Box 790
Claremont, CA 91711
(714) 624-7711
(714) 626-1483
Director, Beverly P. Benjamin, Ph.D.

This 8 week/352 hour course has an additional 6 month supervised probationary work period and a total cost of $1,200 plus expenses. Financial aid is possible. It is registered with the State of California as private post secondary school. Entrance requirements include high school diploma, "significant" childcare work, 3 references, criminal check, 3 psychological tests, TB test and health clearance.

Basic subjects covered include: child development, infant and toddler preschool lab, pediatric health instruction, nutrition, microbiology and food sanitation, fine arts units, social graces, cooking for children, family dynamics, personal appearance, and housewifery skills. First class graduated December 1983.

California Nanny College
2740 Fulton Avenue, Suite 129
Sacramento, CA 95821
(916) 484-0163
Director, Carolyn R. Curtis

This 15 week program has a total cost of $2,000. A $400.00 deposit is required with balance paid in monthly installments following graduation. Financial aid through JTPA funding for local students. Approved by California State Department of Education. Entrance requirements include high school diploma, 3 references, previous child care experience, psychological testing, 2 interviews, and medical clearance.

Subjects covered include: children's nutrition, child development, the atypical infant, infant care, health, safety, and first aid, creative play, employer/employee relations, effective parenting, assertiveness training, family structure and dynamics, personal growth and development, field placement seminar, field placement in nursery or day care center. First class graduated January, 1984.

CAPE Center, Inc.
(Childcare Alternatives and Parent Educ.)
5952 Royal Lane, Suite 161-A
Dallas, Texas 75230
(214) 692-0263
Directors, Janet Spence and Judith Schneider

This course consists of 200 hours class time, and a 50 hour practicum. The course may be taken full time over a

4 month period, or part time over a 6 month period. The total cost is approximately $1000. Deferment of tuition or a time payment plan is available. The center is now seeking accreditation with the Texas Licensing Association. Entrance requirements include high school degree, and a minimum 18 years old. (For placement upon graduation, students must have references, psychological evaluation, good driving record, and police check.)

Basic subjects covered include: child development, behavior management, nutrition, safety, first aid, CPR, record-keeping, family dynamics, general psychology, appropriate learning activities for children, and play. First class graduated June, 1985.

Career Specialists Institute
3300 Monroe Avenue
Rochester, N.Y. 14618
(716) 385-9850
Director, Linda Underhill

This full-time, 15 week course has a total cost of $2000. Financial aid is available through loans and sponsorships. Entrance requirements include high school diploma, physical and psychological screening, references, and interview. The course is accredited by the New York Department of Education.

Basic subjects covered include: childhood growth and development, child psychology, educational activities, first aid, CPR, care of the sick child, nutrition, household management, independent business. First class graduates November, 1985.

Chaffey College
5885 Haven Avenue
Alta Loma, CA 91701
(714) 987-1737
Coordinator of Childcare Development, Debra Davis, Ph.D.

This course runs for 2 years, full-time. For California residents, the cost is $35 per quarter, and for out-of-state residents, the cost is $60 per quarter. Students are eligible for federal aid. Entrance requirements include direct application to and acceptance from Chaffey College. The course is accredited by the Community Colleges of California.

Basic subjects covered include: Introduction to careers with children, child study and observation, child growth and development, the child with special needs, child/family and community, the child in a multi cultural society, field work, administration of a safe and health environment, nutrition, home management, parent/child interaction, and infant/toddler development.

Child Care Specialists Center, Inc.
9533 Brighton Way
Beverly Hills, CA 90210
(213) 274-2653
Directors, Janice Anderson and Sandra Lewis

This 4-week full-time course with a 6-week part-time follow-up (one night a week while working as a nanny) has an $800 fee. A deposit of $200 is required at the start of the program. The balance is due upon placement in a child care position. The school is accredited through California State Department of Education. Entrance requirements include a minimum age of 18 years old and high school diploma, fluent English skills, childcare experience, driver's license.

Basic subjects covered include: growth and development, health, CPR, daily care and nutrition for infants and toddlers, using community resources, creative play, effective behavioral management, art and music appreciation, empathy training, medical and emotional disorders of children. First class graduated June, 1985.

Delta College Nanny Program
Delta College
University Center, Michigan 48710
(517) 686-9543
Director, Joy Shelton

This full-time 10 week training course has several tuition rates: $1112.75 in-district, $1583 out-district, $919.25 senior citizens, and $1953.50 out-of-state. Some financial aid is available. Entrance requirements include general college admissions, plus a personal interview.

Basic subjects covered include: families in American culture, child growth and development, infant and toddler care, family communication, health care, nutrition, travel and exploring community resources, etiquette and dress, negotiating a contract, and field work. First class graduated Fall, 1983.

Development Center for Nannies
500 E. Thomas St.
Pheonix, AZ 85012
(602) 279-3067
Co-directors: Kathy Parker, Dr. Margaret Barcley

This course includes 130 hours of training over a 12 week period. Forty hours are done in class, and ninety in at-home modules. Tuition, $500 for in-state residents and $700 for out-of-state residents, and may be paid in installments. The course is accredited as a licensed private school by the State of Arizona. Entrance requirements include: psychological examination, interview, and a demonstrated love of children.

Basic subjects covered include: child development, nutrition, communication, home management, environmental safety, CPR, and first aid. First class graduated July, 1984.

J. Seargent Reynolds Community College
Downtown Campus
Demonstration Child Care Center
P.O. Box C-32040
Richmond, VA 23261-2040
(804) 786-7602
Directors, Susan O'Brien, Martha L. Green

This course covers 3 college quarters (49 college credit hours) and costs $882.00 ($18 per credit hour). Financial aid opportunities are many and varied. This course has the State of Virginia certification. General college admissions policy, with interview prior to program enrollment, and board interview prior to internship.

Basic subjects covered include: observation techniques, child growth and development, behavior management, language arts, first aid and safety, experiential/developmental approach to learning, internship. First class graduated September, 1984.

Midway College Nanny: In-Home Childcare
Specialist Program
Midway College, Early Childhood Center
Midway, Kentucky 40347
(606) 846-4421
Director, Kay Emerson Roy

This course runs for 2 years, and costs $3500 per year. Financial aid is available through grants, scholarships, and workstudy; no applicant will be turned away because of financial need. Entrance requirements include submission of ACT scores, good GPA, 3 letters of recommendation, police background check, psychological testing, and a committee interview. The course is accredited by the Southern Association of Colleges.

Basic subjects covered include: liberal arts, literature, language, infant and toddler care, professionalism, child development, health safety, nutrition, in-home childcare, methods and materials, food preparation, swimming, horseback riding, sports for young children. Students receive Red Cross certificate in CPR and infant CPR. (This school is working closely with the Norland Nanny School in England to develop a six months exchange program.) First class graduates May, 1987.

Nannies of Cleveland, Inc.
15707 Detroit Avenue
Lakewood, OH 44107
(216) 521-4650
Director, Monica Bassett, R.N.

This 9-week course has a total tuition of $850 + materials. Tuition deferment is available to qualified students. Approved by the Ohio State Board of School and College Registration. Entrance requirements include high school degree, minimum 18 years old, medical examination, personality assessment, personal interview, 5 references and a good driving record.

Basic subjects covered include: child growth and development, infant and child care, health and safety, nutrition, care of the sick child, certified CPR and first aid, creative play and learning, children with special needs, interpersonal relationships, family life, home management, personal and professional development, and a practicum of experience in child care centers. First class graduated August, 1985.

Nanny Child Caring Plan, Inc.
11505 22nd Avenue South
Burnesville, MN 55337
(612) 894-2734
Director, Jacquline Richardson, Ph.D.

This 8-week course has a total cost of $1,277.50. Financial aid may take the form of $50 weekly during the nanny's training internship. The course is currently applying for a State of Minnesota license for vocational and private schools. Entrance criteria include minimum age of 18, high school diploma or GED Equivalent, a good driving record, evidence of ability to work with children, references, criminal check, and a statement of good health from a physician.

Basic subjects covered include: child growth and development, discipline and guidance, the pre-school child, family dynamics/communication, health/safety, nutrition, homemaking for children, infant care with lab practicum, professionalism and the role of the nanny. First class graduated in June 1985.

Nanny U
2253 Giddings
Chicago, IL 60625
(312) 334-2269
Directors, Pat Kovar and Linda Polk

This 12 week course (or more; length depends on full time or part time status) costs $1,000. The only financial assistance is half payment upon matriculation and half payment before graduation. Currently seeking State Board certification. Entrance requirements include high school diploma, minimum 18 years old, extensive screening (including psychological testing), criminal check, and reference checks.

Basic subjects covered include: Child growth the development, creative activities and play, interpersonal skills, health, nutrition and safety, business negotiations, and practicum. First class graduates, Spring 1986.

National Academy of Nannies, Inc.
3665 Cherry Creek Drive North, #320
Denver, CO 80209
(303) 333-NANI
Director: Teresa S. Eurich

This course involves 1,043 hours of training in the form of 4½ months of academic, and 3 months of practical training. The total cost of this course is $2,325. Financial aid, in the forms of private loans and deferred tuition plan are available. The course has been accredited by the Colorado State Board for Community Colleges and Occupational Education, and the U.S. Department of Immigration and Naturalization Services to accept and train foreign students. Entrance requirements include high school diploma or GED, 5 recommendations, acceptable driving record and completed medical form, and extensive psychological screening.

Basic subjects covered include: Child development and child psychology, nutrition, safety, health care, extensive employee relations, and infant, toddler, pre-school and school age childcare labs. The first class graduated in January, 1984.

New England School for Nannies
41 Baymore Drive
East Longmeadow, MA 01028
(413) 525-1861
Director, Karen Hamlin

This 10-week/140 hour course has a total cost of $900 and is offered in both Boston and Springfield, Massachusetts. Financial aid is available through client-sponsored tuition. Out of town students are provided with host families at no cost, taking care of room and board needs. It is licensed by Massachusetts Department of Education. Entrance criteria include application and references.

Basic subjects covered include: first aid and CPR,

growth and development from newborn to adolescence, educational play, child safety, the role and responsibility of the nanny, how to raise a responsible child, First class graduated July, 1985.

North American Nannies, Inc.
61 Jefferson Avenue
Columbus, Ohio 43212
(614) 228-6264
Director, Judith Bunge, Ph. D.

This course is either 8 or 12 weeks, depending primarily on previous college education. Cost is $975 for the 8 week program or $1,350 for the 12 week program. Tuition loans are possible. The course is accredited by the Ohio State Board of School and College Registration. Entrance requirements include minimum 18 years of age, high school degree, personal interview, national police and credit check, psychological assessment and experience as a child care provider.

Basic subjects covered include: infant care, theories of child development, safe and healthy environments for children, creative learning experiences appropriate to each developmental level curriculum, art, music, pre-math and pre-science activities, the role of play, guidance and discipline, personal growth and development, effective skills in working with families. First class graduated November, 1984

Seattle Central Community College
The Certified Nanny Program
Early Childhood Education Department
1701 Broadway, Seattle, WA 98122
(206) 587-6900
Director, Gloria Myre

This course is 3 college quarters long, plus 3 to 6 months field supervision. The resident cost is $230 per quarter (total cost, $851). Grants and scholarships are available. It is accredited by the State of Washington. Entrance requirements include high school diploma or GED, CGP reading comprehension, personal interview, and 3 references.

Basic subjects covered include: basic early childhood development, general studies, supervised practicum, health and safety, professionalism, and special nanny-related subjects. First class graduates Winter, 1986.

Training Your Own

While some form of training is essential for quality and professional in-home care, the avenue of training can be adjusted to meet the individual family or nanny's needs. Intelligent, sincere, and child-loving candidates are rare enough before adding a training prerequisite. Because of this scarcity, many families have decided to "train their own." Training your own nanny can be easy and relatively inexpensive, and cover much of the same basic curriculum as a nanny training school—minus perhaps the etiquette and employer/employee relations (which are often learned on the job anyway). While the nanny may not have all that would constitute a nanny degree when she finishes her individual training, she can be trained to a specific family's needs and therefore perform as a professional in that household. To train their in-home childcare providers, many families use local resources such as the Red Cross, public libraries or bookstores, and community colleges. Listed below are different training options that community resources might offer.

The Red Cross

The Red Cross offers much more than just the traditional first aid training, and of course their reputation is unbeatable. Subjects which the Red Cross has courses in include several variations of first aid—from basic to emergency, all levels of swimming and lifesaving, family health, home nursing, preparation for parenthood (also possible for nannies "expecting" newborns), and much more of value to the nanny in training. Call your local chapters for course lists and times. (NOTE: Not all chapters have courses on all of the above subjects.)

Community Colleges

Community colleges are within 50 miles of almost any home. Most have programs offering degrees in childcare related fields, such as child development, day care assistant, or child care worker. Tuition at these schools is usually quite reasonable. Taking some or all of the offered courses will increase the nanny's knowledge and professional status. Each college has different names for it's courses, and each school will have it's own areas of specialization. I randomly chose two community colleges and listed their major required courses in the child care related degree program.

Child Development For Childcare Workers
Planning A Curriculum For Child Care
Children's Literature
Science And Math For Young Children
Language Arts For Young Children
Expressive Arts For Young Children
Social Development In Young Children
Planning And Administering Childcare Programs
Developmental Tasks For Preschool Children
Introduction To Exceptional Children
Fostering Children's Comminication Skills
Creative Activities For Preschool Children
Current Issues In Childcare
Child Care Practicum And Workshops

With the tremendous increase in courses offered on

community college cable television stations, many nannies can even earn credits evenings or weekends at home.

Public Libraries And Bookstores

Books offer a wealth of training which can be taken in at the nannies leisure. Many families ask their nannies to read books which reflect specific childrearing philosophies. The child related books available number in the thousands, including everything from infant nutrition to safety proofing the home. You will need to decide which books you feel are of quality and worth your time. For suggestions, ask your family pediatrician or the local birth education center.

If you are interested in a specific area of study, but cannot take a course in the subject, simply go to a local college bookstore and pick up the required texts for that course which meet your interests. You do not have to be a registered student to buy these books.

Other Resources

With the increase in home video programs, you can also order tapes on a variety of child related subjects. Also check your local YWCA, YMCA, and birth education centers (Lamaze training centers) as they often have courses which would be educationally beneficial to the nanny in training.

CHAPTER 6

WHAT EVERY NANNY SHOULD KNOW

Who Makes A Good Nanny?

M any different kinds of people make good nannies. I have successfully placed both the quiet and "bubbly" personalities, those in their twenties and those in their fifties, and while some have had only a High School education, others have had advanced degrees. There are, however, certain personality traits which individuals who make good nannies have in common. If you are considering becoming a nanny, I suggest that you assess your personal strengths and weaknesses with those I have listed below. If you find that you have many of the strengths I mention, you will probably be a very good nanny, and therefore enjoy the profession.

NANNIES "MOST LIKELY TO SUCCEED" WILL HAVE:

Integrity—A good nanny will have a strong sense of integrity. She says what she does, and she does what she says. She holds firm in her principles, and keeps the commitments she makes. This integrity may come from her upbringing, religion, high self-esteem, or a combination of all three. Wherever it comes from, it is evident in her every day life.

Self-Esteem—Positive self-esteem is essential for the nanny. She must feel comfortable with her rights as a professional and as a human being. However, self-esteem should never be confused with arrogance, which is in fact a sign of low self-esteem. The nanny with a positive self-esteem will have a balance of flexibility and firmness in her working/living arrangements.

Patience—Everlasting patience is the most important virtue in a nanny. Children require more patience than almost any person has, so it is important for the nanny to have more than the average amount.

An Explorer Mentality—The nanny who has a sense of adventure, who likes to explore life and its wonders, is wonderful with young children. This nanny will not become impatient or bored with a child's inquisitive nature. In fact, she will receive more personal and professional rewards from her position because she is not only leading in the education of a child, she is journeying with him!

A Sense of Humor—The nanny *must* have a sense of humor. Children will be children, and mud pies on a new sweater, broken vases, and crayon pictures on the bedroom wall are all part of the territory. Those nannies who can laugh (at least inside) at such incidents will fare much better than those who take them too seriously.

An Active Personality—Nannies need to be, and need to like to be, very active. Children are always on the go, and nannies need not only to keep up, but lead the way!

Self-Motivation—Most nannies are their own supervisors throughout the day. Those who are not self-motivated enough to plan an active day for their charges will be performing more as babysitters than childcare professionals. Those who have the qualifications to perform as a childcare professional, but need outside motivation to do so, would likely be best in a more structured working environment.

Empathy Skills—Empathy skills are the first step to a personal relationship with the children a nanny cares for. A lost dog or broken toy can be devastating to a child, and a nanny must genuinely feel for her charges in order to build a sound and secure relationship as the child's surrogate parent.

A Cheerful Disposition—Children are happy when there are happy people around them. Those with a truly positive outlook on life and a cheerful attitude daily make the kind of nanny children (and their parents) like most!

A Level Head—Emergencies abound with children. The good nanny will keep a level head in emergencies. She will also have the good judgement to know when she should make decisions on her own, and when she should contact her employers for advice first.

Maintaining A Personal Life While Living In

For the live-in relationship to be a long-term and happy one, nannies need to develop a personal life outside of the home. This includes both time alone and time with friends. Even the nanny who is considered a member of the family needs her own life when off-duty. I offer the following suggestions to nannies to help maintain a personal life while living in an employer's home:

1)   Insist on private accommodations; at minimum a private bedroom and shared bath. It is preferable that they be located on a separate floor or wing than the rest of the family's bedrooms, so that you feel you have a place of retreat. Accommodations which feature a separate entrance, private sitting room or ultimately a completely private apartment should be highly valued.

2)   Whatever your accommodations are, make a *home* out of them. Decorate with personal items; even furnishing your accommodations yourself if you like and are allowed. Try to get a large comfortable chair or loveseat if possible. The place you sleep and the place you relax to listen to music or read should not always have to be the same. Your home-within-a-home will be your haven, and the one thing you will not have to share with the rest of your employing family.

3)   Request that your private accommodations be off-limits to the rest of the family, unless invited by you. Children do not always understand what "off-duty" means. If your accommodations are always off-limits to them, you have at least one place of retreat when you want to be alone.

4)   Develop outside interests, both on your days off and after work in the evenings. These interests should include both friends and activities. (Washington, D.C. has a nanny network. Those not in the D.C. area could form one in their community.) Some families encourage an evening course at a community college, or perhaps you would enjoy ushering at a community theatre. While many times these interests will need to be flexible to unexpected job demands, they will be your saving grace when you really need a change of scenery.

5)   Try to negotiate the requirement of eating dinner with the family daily (unless of course you have your days free while the children are in school and/or working to the children's bedtime is in your job description). Employers usually expect nannies who share the dinner hour to either help with, or completely take care of, the after-dinner dishes. For late dining families (very common in two parent professional families), by the time the nanny is completely free to go it can be 9 p.m.! Most nannies have a long enough day without having to work beyond the time

her employers return home. Needless to say, this requirement also deters any kind of weekday social life.

6) Make sure you have relationships outside of the home. Everyone has personal problems and a right to them, but your employer is not the person to share them with. Unloading on your employers make them feel both resentful, at and responsible for, making your personal life more happy. This is too large a burden for the delicate in-home relationship. Of course, you *should* discuss any work-related problems with your employers (and in fact these problems should *not* be discussed with outside friends).

7) Understand from the onset that your employers home is not *your* home. You will probably not be able to invite guests over without permission, and male friends will not always be welcome in your private accommodations. You must find alternate solutions to these socializing needs.

8) Maintain a private phone line if at all possible. Employers who go to bed before you cut off incoming calls will not likely be pleased at having to run three flights of stairs to tell you that you have a phone call. It is also easier to deal with long distance phone calls and calls you wish to be lengthy. Some families even provide a private phone and pay for the basic (but not long distance) phone charges as part of their benefit package.

9) Get away from the house on your days off and vacation. It is too tempting for employers to ask you for "a little help" if you are around. If you comply, you may end up feeling you have not had your day off or vacation at all. If you do not, your employers may feel you are inflexible. In addition, the change of scenery is essential for a positive outlook on life when your workplace and home is one in the same.

The Resume for the In-Home Position

Like any other professional, nannies should have a resume. However, because the nanny is searching for far more than a nine-to-five office job, her resume should be designed to include both a professional history and important personal information. A compatible personality is a large percentage of what families are looking for. Therefore, the nanny should not be afraid for her resume to project a strong reflection of her personality and style.

The following suggestions and sample resume is in the form which have most impressed my clients. From this basic sample, the individual nanny should creatively apply her individual style.

Start with a cover letter. This letter should be addressed to each individual family with whom you are applying for a position. The cover letter should include the following: 1) A short, basic introduction of yourself and how the job was discovered; 2) Explanation of your current working situation, and when you are looking to begin a new position; 3) A short paragraph concerning why you are interested in, and feel you would be good for the position; 4) A means of reaching you for interviewing; and 5) Appreciation for their consideration.

The actual resume should include, at minimum, the following; 1) full name, 2) address, 3) phone, 4) date of availability, 5) Social Security number, 6) education, 7) experience and 8) preferences of age, gender, and/or number of children you would like to work with, if any. When listing education and experience, be sure to include highlights which would pertain to the in-home position and relationship.

Attach photo copies of at least three written references, (never give originals) including address, phone numbers, the best time for them to be reached for further questions, relation to the reference, and number of years known.

With this in mind, a selling cover letter and resume might look as shown on pages 74 & 75 .

Developing Good Interviewing Skills

Every nanny will have her own style of presenting herself in an interview. As in her resume, she should feel free to let her true personality show through. The last thing you as a nanny want to do is to give an impression of "the perfect Mary Poppins," and then have to live up to this unrealistic image you have created for yourself. If a family doesn't want to hire you after meeting the real you, you are best to know it in advance.

This does not mean you should not present yourself as a professional in your interviews. Hopefully, a professional presentation *will* show your real style. If the nanny interviewing process is new to you, however, it is understandable that you might not know exactly how to dress, what to ask, etc... for your first interview. For an impressive interview presentation I offer the following suggestions:

1) Once you begin submitting applications and sending resumes, make yourself and those who live with you aware of the way your home phone is answered. You will not be impressive if you or a family member answers your phone with "Shelly's pool hall." A curteous "hello" and "one moment please" or "this is she" will do wonders for the first impression you give.

2) When going to an interview, be sure to be prompt, and make sure to call if you have to cancel or must be late. If you are unsure of directions or the length of time it will take to get to the family's home, make the trip once before the actual interview. If for any reason you *are* late, promptly apologize. Remember, you are taking valuable time in busy lives and wasting it deserves an apology.

3)   Be prepared in an interview. Have your resume with you, with a copy for the interviewer to keep for later review. Have at least three written references with you as well. Be sure to have the phone numbers of the references written on them so your interviewer can double check them (a common practice of good interviewers).

4)   Be dressed nicely; not overdressed or underdressed. I have found that, in the nanny profession, the best impressions are made in classic, simple dresses with low heels, not business suits. While jeans are always unimpressive, in the summer a nice (again simple) blouse with walking shorts and topsider-style shoes can give a cheerful, active impression. Most important, no matter what the style of dress you choose, have a clean and neat overall appearance you will be off on the right foot.

5)   When at an interview, take an active interest in the children. Discussions of salary, accommodations, and days off are necessary, but will be of no importance if the family feels this is all you are concerned with. When you meet the children, ask to hold the baby, talk to the three year old, ask the six year old what he would like his new nanny to be like, etc... Parents will evaluate how their children respond to you, and if there is no interaction you can not expect a favorable impression. (This is also your chance to see if *you* like the children.)

6)   Ask questions about the family's child rearing and discipline philosophies. Express your philosophies and practices, making sure to discuss your ability to be flexibility when these practicies differ with your employers. This conversation establishes your professional status, and therefore is one of the best ways to favorably impress your interviewer.

7)   Before leaving, make the family aware of your time table for making a decision, and let them know where you can be reached for further discussion or the arrangement

of a trial period. Do not expect an immediate offer, but if you are very interested in the position they are offering, feel free to make that known (everyone likes to be liked—even interviewing families).

8) If you don't hear from the family within the time frame that you had agreed upon, feel free to call and ask about their status. This lets you know whether they need more decision time or that they have already hired someone else.

Screening Families

The live-in nanny position is not just a job; it is a relationship. Therefore, every nanny has the right—and the responsibility—to screen a prospective family. However, screening families is more difficult than screening nannies. Most first-time nannies do not know what families who hire nannies are like, and what they should screen for. While it is difficult to explain how to screen for family personaliy and lifestyle, I offer the following suggestions to help at least screen for potential problem situations. Keep in mind that beyond these pitfall areas are basic personality types which either will or will not get along with the individual nanny's personality. This judgement of compatibility can only be made by the nanny, trusting her own good jugdement.

1) The most important thing for a nanny to understand when screening a family is this: *If a family has personal, financial, or household needs which they put aside to hire a professional nanny, it is very common in times of stress, or dissatisfaction, for them to forget their original agreement, imposing their ideal agenda on the nanny with or without her agreement.* I suggest you ask the individual family what their *ideal* household situation would be if they could have whatever they felt most comfortable with. If the family's ideal is quite different from what you are proposing, you will most likely

July 14, 1985

Mr. and Mrs. Michael Allen
1122 Adison Lane
Norfolk, VA 22222

Dear Mr. and Mrs. Allen:

My name is Susan Johnston and I am interested in the position you have advertised in the Washington Post today. I am a 21 year old single female with an Associates Degree in Early Childhood Development. I am currently working in a day care center in my home town of Williamston, Michigan and am looking for a career move in September of this year.

I was attracted to your position because of my sincere enjoyment of twins (I have cared for twins in a long term situation and am a twin myself) which I understand you have two sets of. I feel my education in the child development field, as well as my experience with several children at once through the day care center could benefit your obviously demanding, but enjoyable position.

If after reviewing my resume you are interested in a personal interview, I could be available to spend a trial weekend with your family after an initial phone interview. It is best to reach me at home in the evenings at (555) 555-5555 as my current employers are not yet aware of my intentions to make a career change.

Thank you for your consideration.

Sincerely,

Susan Johnston

SUSAN JOHNSTON

111 Farmington Lane
Williamston, MI 33333
(555) 555-5555

Birth date: 10/28/64
Height/Weight: 5'3"; 125 lbs
Marital Status: Single

Objective: To secure a position in a childcare setting: school, or agency, corporation, or home, using my talents and education to promote the physical, emotional, and intellectual development of children.

Education: Any College
Williamston, Michigan

8/81-5/83   Degree: A.A.
Graduated: May, 1985
Major: Early Childhood Development

Professional Affiliations: National Association for the Education of Young Children, Member

Experience:

1/84-8/85   **INTERNSHIP**—Williamston Child Development Center

7/83-4/84   **INTERNSHIP**—Williamston Child Development Center—Learned about child care center management under director of Center. Helped plan schedules of daily activities, meals, snacks, and rest period. Managed center one day each week.

1/83-5/83   **TEACHER'S AIDE**—Williamston Elementary, Williamston, Michigan—Responsible for working with children with learning disabilities. Developed learning packages for this group, focusing on the major learning problems I had identified. One child was "graduated" to an average learner's group as a direct result of one-on-one tutoring.

2/81-11/82   **CHILDCARE**—Dr. and Mrs. Alex Smith—Cared for infant twin girls afternoons on a daily basis. Responsible for physical care as well as for providing learning experiences.

4/80-10/82   **CHILDCARE**—Mr. and Mrs. Tom Welch—Responsible for care of 4-yr. old and 6-yr. old on weekend days. Activities like registering for library cards and using them regularly were common under my direction.

have some kind of conflict about this at some point in the relationship. A common example would be that of a family who offered to hire a housekeeper one day a week in order to get a professional nanny (as professionals rarely will do heavy housework). This can put a great deal of stress on the family in both finding a reliable house-keeper, and affording her in addition to the nanny's salary. When problems with the housekeeper arise, the employer, now settled in with the new nanny, may require her to take over the housekeeping responsibilities. The nanny is then left with the options to refuse and possibly get fired, do the work and resent it, or quit and have to begin the family search again. (This is not to say that these employers are always ogres. In most cases, the stresses of childcare, housekeepers, more than full-time careers, and a family to spend time with are more than the average person can handle. Even the employer who is basically a **nice person can impose unfair agendas on their nanny when they are feeling over-stressed**).

2)   If the family you are screening has had former nan-nies, insist upon speaking with them alone. You have every right to get references on a family. Many families with prior bad experiences will not want you to talk to former nannies. If they flat out refuse to give these references, (especially if there have been several nannies, none of which they will let you speak with) then refuse to consider them further as, they are probably not good employers to work for.

3)   When speaking to a former nanny, ask about person-ality traits of the family. Are they consistent in childrearing plans? Do they support their nanny's efforts? Do they pay on time, and pay for overtime when they are supposed to? Did they change the job description once she moved in? There will be negative and positive attributes in every fam-ily, and most prior nannies are very honest about the

pitfalls. You will have to decide if the pitfalls she mentions are ones you are willing and able to deal with. Remember, the in-home relationship is difficult, and personality conflicts are common. If the nanny can say nothing good about the employer, but really has few good examples of what was wrong, then you have probably received an emotional (and therefore invalid) reference.

4)   Screen for the family's attitudes toward your interpersonal relationship. If the family seems to want a servant, you must be prepared to be treated like one. If the family wants the nanny to be like a member of the family, yet you are a very private person, your interpersonal expectations may be too great. Find a family who wants a relationship as close to what you want. (First time nannies should keep in mind that being a member of the family is nice, but not to the point of keeping you from a personal life as well. Look for a balance here.)

5)   Screen for the family's attitudes towards salary. Are they negotiating for the lowest possible price and yet the greatest amount of hours and responsibilities? Are they able to comfortably pay the price you can professionally command, or are they really struggling to do so? In either case, I would not recommend working for these potential employers. The first family will most likely push you beyond your original agreement, while the second family (although probabily very nice) will resent your putting such a crunch on their personal finances. Look for a family who is willing and able to pay what you are worth, and to consider increases when they are merited.

6)   Ask about future children. If you don't enjoy working with infants, or are unqualified to handle them, you may find yourself out of a job when a new child comes along. On the other hand, even if you love infants, find out if and how your job description will change when another baby comes along.

7)   Assess the family's attitudes toward outside activities, field trips, etc...with the children. Are these activities encouraged? Is there in fact a budget for this? Some families prefer that the nanny not take the children anywhere in a car, and therefore activities can be limited to arts and crafts at home and walks to the neighborhood park. As a nanny you must be content with whatever constraints a family puts on you if you accept their position, so it is best to know what they will be in advance.

8)   Discuss the family's attitudes toward your personal life. Is it encouraged, even to the point of occassionally accommodating your personal plans? Are your friends welcome in the home when off-duty? Is there a curfew on working days? (If so, I would not accept the position. You are a professional, not a child.) Ask whatever questions you need to to be satisfied that you will have an acceptable personal life.

9)   Be sure you are looking at the same length of time for a commitment. I do not feel a first time nanny should ever lock herself into more than a two year commitment, and usually one year is best. Life changes for everyone, and a broken two year commitment is far worse than a twenty month stay after a one year commitment was made.

When Early Termination of a Commitment is Acceptable

There is nothing more distressing to me than a tearful call from a nanny wanting to quit her position, yet not wanting to break her commitment. Unfortunately, nannies are often too easily intimidated and don't stand up for their rights. Adding to this problem, employers are almost always wealthier, more professionally respected, and older than the nannies they employ. Many nannies, new to the in-home relationship and dealing with this kind of employer, are unsure what—if any—personal and professional rights they have.

The contract (see contracting on page __) between a nanny and a family is meant to prevent the taking advantage of one party by another. I stress to nannies the importance of a contract if for no other reason than this: **the contract is the only ticket out of a bad position without feelings of failure and the loss of self-respect.** When a family and nanny write a contract together, each acknowledges the hours, expectations, and compensation which they have come to an agreement on. Without a contract, a family can change any of these agreements and leave the nanny without proof of the original agreement.

With a contract, a nanny has two options for any changes an employer has imposed. 1) Negotiate the change to mutual satisfaction; or 2) Refuse the change, as it was not what was agreed to when accepting the position. In this case the nanny may be writing her own resignation. (She may in fact *prefer* the position to end. However, to maintain her professionalism she must first give her employers the chance to return to their orginial contracttual agreement before leaving the position.)

In addition to the direct breaking of a contract, I do not believe a nanny needs to keep a commitment in the following instances: 1) If the family has taken advantage of her lack of knowledge of what is fair to demand of a nanny. For example, I have seen a college graduate work for $75.00 per week, including in the job description 15 hours a day and full housework. She was unaware that her education and prior experience entitled her to a professional's salary, much more reasonable hours, and only light housekeeping duties. However, the family was aware of this, and in fact made the nanny feel very guilty for breaking a commitment because they knew they would not be so lucky next time. 2) If conditions on an interpersonal level are unbearable. An example of this could be an alcoholic employer who rages when he/she drinks, insulting or even attacking the nanny as a person or professional. Another example might be a jealous or insecure mother who constantly finds fault in the nanny's work to make herself feel she still is the better "mother" in the home.

It is important for the nanny to understand that along with the rights of a contract and a fair working and living arrangement, she has the responsibility to keep her commitments if the family keeps theirs. It is not acceptable to leave a position before the commitment has been fulfilled because the nanny is tired of it, because a good career opportunity arises, or because a slightly better or more interesting position is offered. As a professional, the nanny's first concern must be her charges. Job-hopping creates feelings of inconsistency and sometimes even trauma for children (not to mention their parents) who have lovingly bonded to a nanny. In addition, for *whatever* reason a nanny leaves, a minimum of two, if not four weeks notice must be offered to the employing family. The family may choose not to use this notice, but a professional nanny will at least offer it.

Professional Safeguarding

The American nanny as professional is only beginning to come of age. Along with our pioneering efforts comes a responsibility to make the profession one to be honored and respected. This means safeguarding (i.e. protecting through safety) the nanny's image and role in the American society.

The media are very attentive to nanny issues. This is helping to raise the public awareness and therefore the status of the in-home chilcare provider. However, at the same time, they also give heavy coverage to child abuse and kidnapping issues as well. It has been said that there is nothing the media would like more than to cover both the newly emerging nanny profession and child abuse or kidnapping issues at the same time; that it would make a great—albeit tragic—story. Besides the personal tragedy for the individual family and nanny, nothing would discredit the newly emerging nanny profession more than such an occurrence.

Let me first discuss professional safeguarding in the case of kidnapping. It is likely that many nannies will work for wealthy and/or politically active families. Both are high risks for kidnapping. Nannies working for single parents also run the risk of kidnapping from the spouse who does not have custody. While a kidnapping could happen while anyone is caring for a child, nannies are paid to be responsible for their charges. Any nanny that is not realistic about the dangers for children today and does not take the responsibility for safeguarding her charges is *not* a professional.

Many nannies may not understand that a child of a high risk family is in any danger. While not necessarily careless, this nanny may not be as cautious as she needs to be. It is essential for your professional well-being as a nanny that you know the kind of dangers your charges could be in, and how their parents wish them to be protected from them. If a parent has problems, for example, with wandering through shopping malls or leaving the child in a library's children's section while you browse in another section, you must respect these concerns and follow their wishes.

Child abuse, especially sexual abuse, is a highly emotional issue. As we have seen far too frequently, a childcare workers are not immune to being child abusers. Parents can be greatly reassured by a nanny who has had a criminal record check done prior to employment. (See page 40 for information on criminal checks) For the nanny, going into a position with proof of a clean record is another sign of a true professional—one that the prospective employers will respect. Keeping a daily log as suggested on page __ both provides parents the opportunity to know what a nanny and child is doing throughout the day, where and when specific bumps and bruises came from (usually normal children's activities), etc. . . and protects the nanny by making the information open for inspection.

There is another child abuse issue of importance to nannies. That is the problem of parents abusing the children in the nannies charge. While many people wish to overlook the realities of child abuse, the statistics show that one out of every four girls and one out of every seven boys are abused before they are 18 years old. Statistics also show at least 40% of the abusers are fathers, step-fathers, or men in the father role.[1]

Besides the obvious, some problems can occur for the nannies in this instance. One can be that the nanny is blamed or even set up to look like she is the abuser. Another is that in reporting suspicions of child abuse to the authorities, she may very well be jeopardizing her job.

There are precautions for this that nannies can take both before taking a new position as well as when in an existing one. I offer the following suggestions:

1)   Before accepting a position, discuss child abuse and abduction with the family. Ask what forms of prevention are currently being taken to safeguard against this, and if there have been any problems in the past.

2)   Request that one of the recently written books for children on the topics of child abuse, molestation, and abduction be read as a family, with you present. Making the issues open for discussion lets a child know the subject is not taboo for anyone. If a family member, especially a father, stongly opposes this, you may want to seriously

---

[1].**David Finkelhor,** *How Widespread is Child Serial Abuse, Children Today,* Vol. 13, Issue 4, July-August issue 1984.

consider this before taking the position. Books which have been suggested to me include *Private Zones*, by Frances Dayee, for pre-school and kindergarten age children and *No More Secrets For Me*, by Oralee Wachter, which is recommended for children from first through sixth grades. There is also an entertaining video by Paramount Home Video (available thorugh most home video rental stores) called *Strong Kids, Safe Kids*, with Henry Winkler, which is useful for all ages of children.

3) As a professional, keep abreast on the current issues in child abuse, symptons of children who are being abused, and preventative measures which you as a nanny can take. *Just No More Secrets*, by Caren Adams and Jennifer Fay, is written for adults and covers the issues of sexual abuse of children, offering suggestions for it's prevention.

4) If you do seriously suspect child abuse in your current position, contact your local Protective Services (often called other things such as child welfare, etc...and can be found by calling your local Social Services Department.) In doing this, you may risk the early termination of your position. Even with this risk, it is both your moral and professional responsibility to the child you care for to report these serious suspicions. *(Note—sexual abuse is not something children joke about. If a child you care for confides in you that he is being abused sexually—BELIEVE HIM, and report it.)*

Professionalism Within The Home—*Deborah Davis, Ph.D.*

Although much has been published in the literature of child care about the areas of child development, nutrition, and children's health and safety, little is known about the unique area of professional skills required of nannies who work directly in the child's home. How the nanny relates to the whole family and what she needs to know about the finer points of family dynamics is, for her professional success, equally as important as the child development theory. Several points about professionalism come to mind in working with a family in their home:

1) Both the parents and the nanny need to keep private problems to themselves. Unless impending situations have a direct bearing on the welfare of the children, both parties should maintain a respectful distance with regard to intimate details of their personal lives to ensure privacy and a professional relationship. This is not to say that the nanny should not be like a member of the family, but that careful consideration must be made about how intimate this family relationship should become.

2) The nanny and family should be absolutely discreet in discussing *anything* about the nanny or family outside the household. To anyone other than the immediate family the children are perfect angels, the parents are perfect parents, and the nanny is a competent professional. Any differences must be aired at home in the proper setting.

3) Whatever good or bad habits a nanny has, these will be transmitted to the children, just as parental behaviors are learned by children. I remember my three year old saying "damnation!" to his firetruck—I taught him unwittingly. My nannies over the years have taught him to bite his fingernails, snuffle his nose with a loud snort, roar when angry, and spit. Careful screening and good nanny training can prevent many of these unwanted occurances, and those nannies who know they have bad habits should take special care to overcome them before they have been transmitted to the children.

4) Professionalism can be hampered due to the sometimes unconscious expectations the nanny and family have of each other. For example, a very young nanny with an older mother in the family may use behaviors she is unaware of by putting the older female employer in the role of her own mother. Similarily the roles may be reversed with an older nanny employed in a young household, she may find herself "mothering" both the children and the parents. These learned but unconscious behavior patterns can become most dangerous when there has been a problem in the earlier pattern of the childhood of the nanny or the employer and when that problem has not been resolved positively. The more effectively each party can clarify these elements, the better the relationship will work. I recommend Nancy Chodorow's work on mothering as well as the Nancy Friday's work *My Mother/Myself* for nannies to gain awareness of the elements operating in their relationship within their own families and the professional arena.

5) To maintain her professionalism, the nanny must *want* to be a professional. Every nanny needs to ask herself why she wants to do this kind of work. She should question deeply her motives for caring

for someone else's children in a context where she is not the boss of the mothering. The professional nanny must love, support, and nurture someone else's children in someone else's home. Being a good nanny is hard work and if the family placement is not harmonious the emotional tensions are tremendously difficult, particularly in a live-in situation. The nanny must fully understand what she is undertaking and handle her role professionaly for the in-home relationship to be successfull.

Deborah Davis has her Ph.D. in Education and Policy Studies, is an employer of a live-in nanny, editor of the National Nanny Newsletter, and a college professor at Claremont Graduate School and Chaffey College in Alta Loma, California.

CHAPTER 7

MAKING THE
RELATIONSHIP WORK

L et us assume that after reading chapters one through six that the best possible nanny and the most welcoming and appreciative family have found each other. They now become house-mates, parent-mates, dinner-mates, vacation-mates—Do you ever get the feeling the nanny/family relationship is much like a mail-order marriage? Well it is. And like any marriage, it requires a great deal of communication to make it last.

The Family/Nanny Contract

The most important thing any family and nanny can do to make their relationship last is to write a contract (also called agreement) together, and keep it updated. The word "contract" makes families feel secure, yet usually scares nannies. It should do neither. A nanny cannot be legally bound to a position, even with a contract, as it would not be enforceable in court (much like indentured slavery, it is against the constitution). On the other hand, it *can* bind a family. If, for example, a family decides they no longer need a nanny, that nanny can still sue for her salary for the rest of the contracted period. Ways to avoid this if the nanny is being dismissed for cause is to add a clause in the contract that states "If the employee is dismissed for cause the employer will not be bound to any contractual agreements."

While not legally binding a nanny to a position, the contract is still essential in that it is the most important form of communication on the business level. In the contract, both parties come to an agreement on responsibilities, compensation, and other important negotiations. Because the contract is written, it can be referred back to when differences of opinions occur concerning an original agreement. Many families and nannies feel so comfortable together they forego contracting formalities, only to find themselves wishing they had written one when a disagreement begins to threaten their happy family/nanny relationship.

The contract form on pages 101-106 is a thorough list of what, at minimum, should be covered in a final contract. Use it as a draft for the starting contract, and then from there make a final draft, formatting it to meet your individual needs. The final contract should not be made until the nanny has worked a trial period of 2-4 weeks.

Scheduling for Communication

Regular communication beyond the original contract is also essential for a nanny/family relationship to work. The individual family and nanny must create a style of communication that both parties feel comfortable with, and then work to keep it consistent.

When I talk about good family/nanny communication, I do not mean the therapy-style baring of souls. I am refering to an exchange of information in which both the family and the nanny brief each other on pertinent special events and concerns, and ask any questions one or the other might have. This exchange is a daily one and relates primarily to work issues. This positive communication style will also allow either party to bring up work-related personal issues, problems or concerns in a non-pressured environment of discussion, not accusation or threat. This may occur in a structured, specifically allotted time for such communication or may be more casual, depending on the formality of the relationship and the ability of both parties to communicate well.

Every family and nanny must keep in mind the individual personality of each person in the relationship, and the communication style he or she uses. While an employer with a law degree may be a great communicator in the courtroom, it is not necessarily true that he or she is a good communicator at home with a nanny. Nonetheless, this will be his or her style, and each person (including the lawyer!) in the relationship must learn to work with it. (Note that this is no different than in any other relationship. Many of us can remember knowing the difference between a good and bad time to have a discussion with a parent or spouse, and how to best approach them.)

SUGGESTIONS FOR POSITIVE FAMILY/NANNY COMMUNICATION:

1)   Always remember that *the key to effective communication is to understand that it is preventative medicine, not a symptom-curing drug.* Communication which comes after a major problem can be too late in the delicate family/nanny relationship.

2)   It is best if the family/nanny relationship, no matter how casual or formal, has open communication lines at all times. Many issues cannot wait for an end-of-the-month conference. If major problems are left unresolved for too long, they will often become blown out of proportion by the time they are finally discussed. A general rule of thumb is that no issue should be put off if it makes anyone

in the relationship feel uncomfortable with it being unresolved.

3)   Many families find that a log (as suggested on page 107) and a weekly 45 minute talk over coffee or wine is regular enough. It is often easier than planning 10 minutes at the end of the day when both parties are tired and have other things on their mind.

4)   There should also be a monthly review of personal issues. What personal needs are arising for an individual? Is this interfering with their work or the children? This would be the time, for example, for a mother to make it known that she is approaching an overly hectic month. She can express that due to this work overload, she would like the nanny to make sure to increase her amount of cuddle/talk time with the child to compensate for the mother's increased absence. The nanny, remembering other hectic months before, might then express feelings of possible burn-out by the end of this one. The family might offer a long weekend off at the month's end to give the nanny some recuperating time to look forward to.

5)   A job description and salary review should be planned every six months. (Raises and/or bonuses are a way of communicating appreciation for a job well done or offering a pick-me-up in tough times. Even small incentives mean a great deal to the hard-working nanny.)

6)   When you are communicating, make sure you are not holding a "gripe" session. Updating on the children, including where they are emotionally, physically, intellectually, and socially is important for the nanny and family to discuss together, and is far more constructive than simply complaining to each other for an hour.

7)   When there *are* problems, communicate them in a way which leaves them open for objective discussion. Give specific, recorded examples of the incidences which have

bothered you, and talk about them using "I feel" statements. For example, a nanny may feel offended at being the maid when the family has guests over. The family is likely to argue if the nanny says "I don't want to pick up after your mother." They cannot argue a feeling statement like "I *feel* like I'm more like a maid than a childcare professional when I have to pick up after guests in the house" because *this* is what the nanny is feeling. Once problems are out in the open, offer ideas for solutions to them. For the problem above the nanny might suggest that the parents be responsible to pick up after their guests.

8)   Once problems are discussed, make sure the needed changes are taking place. If they are not, gently but firmly give reminders that you are expecting action.

9)   If no changes occur in the problem areas, even after polite reminders, it is acceptable to provide a rational threat to induce correct behaviors. For example, a nanny who is never paid for overtime hours might say: "I have mentioned several times that I would like to be paid overtime as we originally contracted, and you have agreed to this. However, even after I have provided you an account of these hours, I never get paid for them. The next time you ask for overtime work and do not pay for it I will have to resort to refusing to work any future overtime at all." Another example might be that of a family whose nanny never seems to get the baby's laundry done before the weekend. The family might say: "We recognize that you do not like to do the baby's laundry, but it is in your contract. We have mentioned several times that we have found the baby's clothes are not clean for the weekend on Fridays after you leave. The next time this happens we will insist on proof that the baby's laundry is done before we give you your paycheck on Fridays." Obviously, no one likes to resort to threatening, nor does anyone like to be threatened, no matter how nicely the threat is presented. But it works.

Understanding Each Other's Expectations

As in any relationship, both the family and the nanny will have certain expectations of the working/living arrangement. Some of these expectations will be realistic and others will not. The best way to avoid conflict is to know each others expectations in advance. Each family/nanny relationship has it's own agenda, and the expectations of each party will differ from family to family. However, the following realistic and unrealistic expectations run common in many American family/nanny relationships.

FAMILY EXPECTATIONS WHICH ARE REALISTIC:

Quality Childcare—The American family hires a professional nanny for many reasons, but none so important as the level of quality an educated childcare provider giving one-on-one care can bring. Families expect that the high salaries they pay will afford them the best of care available.

A Smooth Running Home—Parents who work have a hectic enough life without the added pressures of a home in chaos when they return from work each day. Families expect that the agreed upon responsibilities will be performed upon the self-motivation of the nanny, without any need for reminding or coaxing.

A Long Term Relationship—Families want stability for their children and peace of mind for themselves. Families are not interested in those who are using their position as a short term stepping stone to earn a few quick dollars. Families expect commitments to be taken seriously.

Reasonable Interpersonal Expectations—The last thing that parents want is for their nanny to seem like another child in the family, or the responsibility of entertaining a nanny as they would a guest in their home. Families expect the nanny to be mature enough to handle her personal life as a professional nanny would—on her own.

FAMILY EXPECTATIONS WHICH ARE UNREALISTIC:

Fulfillment of the "Housewife Role"—Some families want to fill the empty role of "housewife" now that the mother has returned to work. The housewife role has traditionally been the place to dump all domestic responsibilities, from family errands to serving at parties to cleaning out the refrigerator. While these responsibilities will not go away, they are not to be expected of the professional nanny. Families expecting the nanny to become a dumping ground for any and all extra responsibilities will be disappointed.

On-Call Convenience—Some families feel that because a nanny lives in the home that she is available at the whim of the employer when she is in. A nanny should not have to leave her home just to get some peace from on-call duty. While a live-in nanny is a great back-up in emergencies, she should otherwise know that when her scheduled working hours are over she *will* be finished for the day.

NANNY EXPECTATIONS WHICH ARE REALISTIC:

A Fair Paycheck—The nanny is not so altruistic as to work 12 hours a day only because she loves children. Professional childcare is her chosen profession. No matter how friendly and close she is with the family, she expects a paycheck which reflects her normal salary and any overtime which she has earned.

Only Agreed Upon Responsibilities—A nanny expects that she will be responsible for the duties included in her original job description, not added responsibilities a family chooses to ask of her. Even if she refuses to perform these

93

added responsibilities, she becomes frustrated that she is put in the awkward position of having to refuse, which is uncomfortable for everyone. Nannies expect to do the job they were hired to do.

A Personal Life—Nannies do not expect that because they commit to a live-in position that they forego a personal life, including fair amounts of time off. Nannies expect that their job is a part of their life, not all of it.

Respect As A Professional—The nanny who performs as a professional expects to be respected as a professional.

NANNY EXPECTATIONS WHICH ARE UNREALISTIC:

True Family Member Status—A nanny sometimes wants the love, support, and understanding of her employing family that she found in her real family. Employing families do not want to include the nanny in everything they do, nor do they want to be responsible for another "child's" needs and desires. The professional nanny will understand her limitations as a "family member."

An Easy Job of Glamor—Some nannies who begin working for wealthy families are expecting any easy babysitting job with glamor and world travel. They are not expecting to really work as hard as professional care providers do. These nannies do not last long unless they quickly adjust their attitude.

Independence Without Control—The nanny is often her own supervisor, but this does not mean her employers will not have any control over what she does with her charges. A nanny may expect to plan her work days as she pleases and have a free reign to raise her charges under her own philosophy of childrearing. This nanny will be disappointed when she finds her employers are not giving up their rights as parents just because they hire a professional childcare provider.

Servant Status vs. Part of the Family

Traditionally, the nanny role has had a servant status, along with the housekeeper, butler, chauffuer, etc... While the nanny held a warm and loving place in the hearts of many families, she was nonetheless still of a lower class and considered hired help. However, for most families today, the American nanny role is built on a different concept. Today, it is the middle and even upper-middle class woman deciding to enter the nanny profession. Therefore, the American nanny is not intended to be a servant, but a professional, and in many cases, is even considered to be like a part of the family.

Some families still want the nanny to be perform a servant role; wearing a uniform and speaking when spoken to. This kind of family has the most difficult time finding a professional nanny, as the middle class is not comfortable with such roles. These families often have to resort to the uneducated, lower class individual who is accustomed to the servant role, change their attitudes to accommodate the professional, or pay extraordinary high salaries to get the professional nanny to accommodate their servant role preferences.

Being considered a member of the family is appealing to many families and nannies, and yet has no specific meaning as all families are different. I have found that, in general, most families feel that the term "like a member of the family" implies the following: A nanny is free to roam the house both on and off duty, and is invited into the "common areas" of the house on evenings and weekends to watch T.V., listen to music, etc... While the nanny is not required to eat dinner with the family every night, she is welcome to if she wishes. If the nanny chooses to accompany the family on a weekend outing she would be welcome, but will be expected to help out as any member of the family would. The nanny is personally involved on a friendly basis with all members of the family, with dinner table discussions from politics to salt-free diets to whatever else families talk about at the dinner table. The nanny is required to live by the same basic house rules as everyone else in the home.

Some families and nannies feel most comfortable with a relationship which is not as distant as a servant/employer, yet not as close as a family member would be. The nanny is respected as a professional, yet is still seen as an employee. The accommodations provided for her are to be her home-within-the-home. After-hours and on weekends she is expected to enjoy them, and not the other common areas of the home. She is expected to eat dinner with the children or on her own, as the parents feel they need some private time together. Her guests must be announced in advance and introduced upon their arrival.

The specific relationship that develops will depend on the individual personalities of the family and the nanny, and how well they get along. Families should know that in general, if there is a mutual attitude of respect towards each other as professionals and as human beings, most nannies are satisfied with their in-home relationship, whatever the specific ground rules are. If there is not, most nannies see the position as a quick way to make money, and are rarely committed to the job if something better comes along.

Socio-Economic Differences

One day, about two weeks after I had made a placement between a family and nanny, I got a call from the nanny. She explained to me that she wasn't sure what she was feeling, but it was some combination of anger, offense, and confusion. She went on to explain that after much negotiation, she took the position at a $25.00 a week cut from what she had expected to start at. She had felt her qualifications entitled her to a specific starting salary, but the family wouldn't offer it. Because she liked them so much, she took the job anyway. Now two weeks later, the mother went on a shopping spree spending $15,000. The nanny could not understand why her employer had haggled over the starting salary, and then went on to spend her *yearly* salary in a day.

This is a problem most middle class nannies must face at some point of their careers with wealthy families. While the traditional servant class knew the etiquette to deal with these socio-economic differences, the ever upwardly mobile middle class does not, and some nannies even have an identity crisis over it. A whole book could be written on the middle class entering a traditionally servant class position, but for the purposes of the nanny, I can only offer her the following ideas:

1) If a situation like above occurs, remember that it is natural to feel confused, even angry. But remember that what you are getting angry about is a way of our culture, not the individual family. Consider the experience a part of learning about the world.

2) As a nanny, you are valued on a market scale, not as a human being. Just because most people could not live without a can opener, that does not mean people will pay $5,000 for one. You will be paid according to both your market value (i.e. your background combined with what nannies earn in your area) and the level of difficulty of the individual position.

3) It is none of your concern how your employers do or do not spend their money, and they will not appreciate your comments or questions. Money is a private matter, and they will not ask how you spend yours.

4) Just because a family lives in luxury, that does not mean you will. For example, when traveling, the family will rarely rent you a hotel suite just because they have one. It sometimes feels like a cold slap in the face, but in the end,

a nanny is an employee and the "part of the family" status often stops at the wallet.

Nanny "Burn-Out"

Job stress can result in burn-out in any profession. In the live-in nanny situation, nannies are especially susceptible to job stress and burn-out because it is difficult to get away from that stress when you live where you work. Even the highest quality and finest trained nanny who is in a happy, long-term family/nanny relationship can be lost to a situation of burn-out.

To prevent burn-out, families and nannies must first understand the stress that produces it. It is important to remember that stress is not always negative. In the work environment, optimal stress results in good performance, decision-making sharpness, good morale, high job satisfaction, alertness, and clear perception. Optimal stress balances directly between work underload and work overload. Work underload (i.e. not enough work challenge) can result in boredom, depression, increased anxiety, reduced job satisfaction, and apathy. Work overload (i.e. too much work or requirements beyond one's capabilities) can result in insomnia, poor job performance, and reduced job satisfaction.[1]

Occasional work underload or overload are inevitable in any profession at different points in time. In fact, a change of pace can help keep a job interesting. However, when underload or overload are the rule, these negative results will occur.

Burn-out and stress prevention for the nanny depends a great deal upon how well the family and nanny can communicate their feelings and needs. Good communication about work overload or underload levels might begin

[1]. *Managing Job Stress and Health,* Michael T. Matteson and John M. Ivacevich, Free Press, N.Y., N.Y., 1982, pp 86.

with a family asking questions such as: What makes you work harder? What makes you feel lazy? Under what conditions might your feel underloaded or overloaded? What might we or our children do to push you past your optimal stress level? How can we help you say "no" if you feel you need to? Is there any training we could give you to help you reduce any anxiety about your performance?

If the nanny is feeling an underload burn-out, families should find ways to channel the nannies abilities and interests to their benefit. The nanny's employers might provide educational research projects, increase the budget for outside activities with the children, or offer that the nanny take in a few neighborhood children the same age as their own to form a playgroup once or twice each week.

If the nanny is feeling the symptoms of an overload burn-out, her employers will find that the only key to salvaging the working/living relationship is for both parties to communicate their needs, and then negotiate a compromise. Each party must define their bottom line—saving only those needs which are absolutely unchangeable, until the nanny is ready to take on more of her original responsibilities again. (If the job is always one of overload, the nanny may never be able to take back all her responsibilities. Families must then decide if they would rather find another nanny more able to handle the full responsibilities—if there is any nanny who can—or live with some extent of compromise indefinitely.)

The Parent/Nanny Mutual Support System

It is very frustrating when a nanny and a parent directly contradict each other in front of a child. In order for both the parent and the nanny to be listened to and respected by a child, as well as for a child to feel there is continuity between his parents and nanny, there must be a mutual support system. There are many kinds of mutual support systems, and each family and nanny will develop one which is best for them after they have worked together for some time. The following ideas on formulating a mutual support system have worked for myself as a nanny and for many of clients since then.

1) You must first decide what you wish for *the child* to perceive about the mutual support system. Will he know that the nanny is an employee required to follow his parent's instruction (note that this can be used negatively by the child to play the nanny and family off each other), or that the family and nanny hold equal power, and that he must listen to who ever is "on-duty" at the time?

2) Decide in advance which decisions are to be made by the nanny and which ones will be made by the parents. While a nanny makes decisions as to the day's activities, the parent will most likely answer questions about the possibility of a child's friend spending the night or the purchasing of new clothes.

3) Discuss what is to occur when both the nanny and parent are working with the children at the same time. Many families have a system in which the nanny looks for a signal from the parent if a decision must be made. A simple shrug from the parent would mean "Whatever you decide is fine."

4) Whoever has the decision making power at any given time should use their best judgement for each individual case. The party who did not make the decision should back her up in front of the child, no matter how strongly they disagree with it at the moment. The time to discuss the decision is later, when the child is not around.

5) If one party strongly disagrees and must let the other know immediately, they should do it in such a way that they are not contradicting each other in front of the child.

For example, a child may have been given an ice cream cone just moments before a mother came home. The child might ask for some cookies from the mother, knowing the nanny would say no. If the mother says yes, the nanny should not contradict her by saying "No, he already had ice cream," but instead say "Don't you think you ought to tell your mother what you already had for a snack?" This gives the mother the information she needed to change her decision and avoid a direct contradiction between the mother and nanny.

Contract or Written Agreement Form

Agreement between _____ (employer) and

_____ (employee).

1. This agreement covers the time period from ___-___-___ to ___-___-___

2. Termination of contract:

  (1) If the employee is terminated for cause, the employer is not bound to this contract, however two weeks severance pay will be given.

  (2) If the employee decides to leave the position, the employee will provide at least two weeks notice. No **severance pay** is required if employer wishes to terminate before the two week period.

  (3) At the time of employee termination, any outstanding bills incurred by the employer on behalf of the employee may be deducted from the employee's pay.

3. This agreement (and any part thereof) may be amended at any time with the mutual agreement and signature of both parties.

4. Review of contract, performance, and salary set for: (Dates)

_____   _____   _____

5. Full time childcare positions require the following responsibilities:(**Add,** drop, or change any of the following statements to fit your individual **needs.**)

  (A) To provide childcare up to 12 hours per day, five days per week, including 2 consecutive days off per week.

  (B) To provide "light housewifery," which means doing the children's laundry, cleaning the children's bedrooms, playroom, and bathrooms, preparing and cleaning-up after children's snacks and meals, running child-related errands and driving the children when and where needed.

(C) To plan and prepare nutritious meals and snacks for children.

(D) To use creative skills in planning activities that promote the physical, emotional, intellectual, and social development of the child.

(E) To comply with parent's discipline and childrearing preferences.

(F) To provide a cheerful and helpful attitude while on duty.

(G) To promote feelings of security and warmth by planning daily cuddle/read/talk time with the child.

(H) To write daily log sheets of events and to confer dialy with parents about special problems, child's newly learned skills, etc., so as to promote good communication with parents concerning child's daytime life.

(I) To provide *reasonable* flexibility in times of emergency or unexpected schedule changes.

(J) To read/review any pertinent literature provided by parents in order to promote broader knowledge of childrearing philosophy, education, child psychology.

(K) To actively participate in understanding the child's special problems and interests, providing solutions to the former, and enhancing the latter.

(L) To provide optimum learning opportunity for the child by communicating with school teachers and coordinating home learning time with school learning time.

6. Additional responsibilities (use following key):

   Key: "1": Employer or hired help other than employee responsible

   "2": Employee responsible on a regular basis

   "3": Employee responsible upon request and not paid additionally for the service

   (A) Children's bedrooms and playrooms
   ____ "picked up"
   ____ bed made daily

   (B) Children's cooking
   ____ breakfast
   ____ lunch
   ____ dinner

   (C) Children's dishes
   ____ breakfast
   ____ lunch
   ____ dinner

   (D) Employer's bedroom and private sitting rooms
   ____ "picked up"
   ____ bed made daily

   (E) Employer's cooking
   ____ breakfast
   ____ lunch
   ____ dinner

(F) Employer's dishes
_____ breakfast
_____ lunch
_____ dinner

(G) Meal planning and shopping for groceries
_____ children's
_____ family's
_____ employee's

(H) Vacuuming
_____ children's beds and playrooms
_____ employee's private accommodations
_____ entire home

(I) Dusting
_____ children's beds and playrooms
_____ employee's private accommodations
_____ entire home

(J) Cleaning of bathrooms
_____ children's
_____ employee's
_____ all in home

(K) Laundry
_____ children's
_____ employee's
_____ family's

(L) Driving
_____ children's activities
_____ child related errands
_____ household errands

(M) General "picking up" of daily mess
_____ after children
_____ after employer

(N) Tutoring (specify)
_____

(O) Periodic "heavy" cleaning as listed:
_____

(P) Other
_____ removing trash
_____ ironing (children's)
_____ ironing (family's)
_____ packing lunch (children's)
_____ arranging child's doctor/dental appts.
_____ taking child to doctor/dental appts.
_____ taking care of sick child
_____ caring for children when travelling

7. Work Schedule
   1. Daily Schedule:

Monday:	_____ to _____	
Tuesday:	_____ to _____	
Wednesday:	_____ to _____	
Thursday:	_____ to _____	
Friday:	_____ to _____	
Saturday:	_____ to _____	
Sunday:	_____ to _____	

Or...up to _____ average hours per day, with the total not to exceed _____ hours per week.

8. Additional hours of work, not accounted for above:
Number of evenings on reserve* _____

*"Reserve evenings" means a set number of evenings during the week when the employee works (at no added compensation) beyond the normal schedule to accommodate the employer's evening engagements (social or business). These reserve evenings are to be used at the employer's discretion, with ample notice given whenever possible.

Any additional evenings or hours (above the reserve evenings) used by the employer will be considered overtime hours, with overtime pay provided. Reserve evenings (can ____) (can not ____) be accumulated. The base salary of the employee (will ____) (will not ____) be docked for non-use.

9. Compensation:

(A) Employer agrees to pay the employee a base salary of $ _____ per week.

(B) Salary is to be paid every _____ covering the period of _____.

(C) Overtime hours (____ are) (____ are not) option to the employee.

(D) Overtime compensation is paid at an hourly rate of $____/hour.

10. "24-hour duty": (defined as the employee having complete and full care for any 24-hour period).

(A) 24-hour duty occurring during two normal work days will be compensated for as follows:

   ____ time and a half pay
   ____ one additional paid vacation day
   ____ Other

(B) 24-hour duty occurring during one or more scheduled days off will be compensated for as follows:

   ____ double time
   ____ one regular day's pay with one addtional paid vacation day
   ____ 2 additional paid vacation days
   ____ Other

11. Out of town duty: (defined as non-optional, regular working responsibilities while travelling with family.)

(A) While specific hours may vary, the number of working hours will not exceed _____ hours per day.

(B) All travel expenses are to be paid by the employer, except those that the employee elects to incur.

(C) Private accommodations (will ____) (will not ____) be provided for the employee.

(D) Hours worked, days off, and compensation levels will be in accordance with the at-home policies (listed in this agreement), unless changes are listed below:

_____

12. Taxes

(A) Employer agrees to pay and file the legal required state and federal taxes, and (will ____) (will not ____) deduct the employee's personal tax.

(B) If employer witholds tax, employer (agrees ____) (does not agree ____) to put withholding amount in escrow account to ensure availablity at tax time.

(C) Employer (will ____) (will not ____) pay employees portion of the legally required Social Security tax as a benefit to the employee.

13. Vacation

(A) Employer agrees to allow the employee _____ week(s) paid vacation to be taken as follows:

    1) ____ as employer desires

    2) ____ after ____ months and before ____ months.

    3) ____ at the end of one year

    4) ____ Other _____

(B) Employee (will ____) (will not ____) be paid full salary while family travels alone.

14. Holidays

(A) Employer agrees to allow the employee the following paid holidays:

_____   _____   _____

_____   _____   _____

15. Health Insurance

    (A) ____ paid by employer

    (B) ____ % of policy up to $____/year paid by employer

    (C) ____ policy offered by employer but not paid by employer

16. Automobile Provided

    (A) ____ for occasional personal use

    (B) ____ for regular use with permission of employer

    (C) ____ for regular use without need for employer's permission

    (D) ____ work related use only

    (E) ____ not offered, but use of employees care for work-related errands will be compensated at _____ cents per mile and will pay _____ monthly towards insurance and upkeep.

17. Room and Board

(A) ____ full board (all meals, snacks, and other foods consumed by employee), plus specially requested items up to $____/week.

(B) ____ food consumed during working hours only, plus additional items up to $____/week.

(C) ____ Employer agrees to provide accommodations up to ____ days per week.

18. Accommodations and Use of Employer's Property

(A) Areas considered the employee's private accommodations are as follows: _____

(B) Such designated areas (are ____) (are not ____) open to any of employee's guests without employer permission.

(C) Such designated areas (will ____) (will not ____) be cleaned by household staff.

(D) "Common areas" are areas open to all and are listed below: _____

(E) Common areas are to be used by employee as follows:
____ at any time
____ whenever not previously occupied by employer or employer's guests
____ whenever employer is not at home
____ only when employee is working

(F) Common areas may be used to entertain employee's guests as follows:
____ at any time
____ when not previously occupied by employer (without permission)
____ when employer is not at home (without permission)
____ with employer's permission only
____ not to be used by employee to entertain guests
____ Other

19. Respect of private areas and private property

(A) Both employers and employee will respect the privacy of the other by knocking, and awaiting invitation before entering any private areas.

(B) Employer has the right to enter employee's private areas; however, advanced notice will be given whenever possible.

(C) All private property requiring special operating instructions will be available for use only after permission and instructions are given.

(D) Private property not to be operated by employer or employee should be listed below:

20. Other benefits offered:

_____
_____

The Nanny Log

Communication of daily events and potential problems is essential for the smooth running household and a positive employer/employee relationship. However, without structure this communication often will break down. This is sometimes due to time and energy constraints at the end of a long, hectic day for both the parents and the nanny. Other times it is due to the inability by one or both parties to communicate well. The nanny log is a solution to this that many nannies and families have found for keeping communication consistent and complete.

The log has other advantages too. It allows the family to keep abreast of daily events, and therefore feel they are more involved in their children's daily lives. It is also a professional safeguard to nannies who want to be able to show how their day was spent, what overtime hours were accumulated, and voice concerns without a "sit down, let's talk" major confrontation.

Set up a chart using a basic spiral notebook. Divide each page into four columns, leaving a space at the top to date each new entry, at the bottom for comments, problems, issues, and questions. Enough space should be left after each comment section for the parents to respond after reading.

Include these four sections:
★ *Planned activities.* These include outings, arts and crafts, special television programs, play group meetings, etc. These activities do not include normal playtime, regular pre-school classes, etc.

★ *Newly-learned skills and new events.* Since parents cannot always be present to participate in new accomplishments and events, it is important to keep a record of these happenings. Nannies should list special events such as a new tooth breaking through, the first steps, or learning a new letter in this column.

★ *Medical irregularities.* This is the column in which to list physical problems, such as excessive rubbing of ears, diarreha, or rashes. This information is important to the physician who needs to know particulars about a problem and it's accompanying symptoms.

★ *Food consumption.* Since a balanced nutritious diet is vital to the well-being of a young child, nannies should record what foods the child eats. Included in this column should also be food offered and refused, or "picked" at.

EXAMPLE

DATE   **(HOURS)***

Activities	New Skills	Irregularities	Food

Comments: _____
_____
_____
_____

NOTE: Those using an hourly pay scale may want to record their hours here, otherwise it can be used for recording overtime hours.

29 1 117

A 29   33   ᚕ   _